TEACHING TO
Diversity

TEACHING AND LEARNING IN THE MULTI-ETHNIC CLASSROOM

Mary Meyers

Addison-Wesley Publishing Company, Inc.

Library of Congress Cataloging-in-Publication Data
Meyers, Mary, 1948-
      Teaching to diversity : teaching and learning in the multi-ethnic
classroom / Mary Meyers.
            p. cm.
      Includes bibliographical referenced.
      ISBN 0-201-55547-6
      1. English language--Study and teaching (Elementary)--Foreign
speakers. 2. English language--Study and teaching (Elementary--
Great Britain. 3. Children of immigrants--Education--Great
Britain. 4. Language and culture--Great Britain. I. Title.
PE1128.A2M49 1994
372.65'21'0440941--dc20   94-137
                                                                            CIP

Cover design by Julian Cleva
Interior design and illustrations by Julian Cleva
Edited by Norma Pettit
Cover photo by Dennis Broughton, Commercial Photography and Visuals Images

Internal photos, except those indicated below, are by Dennis Broughton, Commercial
Photography and Visual Images.
Figures 1.3, 1.4, 1.5, 1.6, 1.7, 1.9, 5.2 (right), and 5.4 (right) by the author; Figures 1.2,
2.2, 5.4 (left), 9.11 (all), 10.4, and 10.5 by Margaret Kean; Figure 3.1 International
News Photos, UPI/Bettmann; Figure 4.4 Ontario Science Centre; Figure 10.3 Canada
Post Corporation.

Printed in the United States of America.

      2 3 4 5 6 7 8 9 10-CRS-98 97 96 95

Published in the United States
and its territories by
Addison-Wesley Publishing Company
ISBN 0-201-55547-6

Contents

To my dad, the rabble-rouser,
and my mom, the peacemaker,
and to Luke — maybe he can be both.

Aknowledgements

Special appreciation and thanks to:

- my friend and colleague Al Sumpter, who always believed in me, and told me so;
- Norma Pettit and Terry Nikkel, my editor and sponsor;
- the Ontario Teachers' Federation and the North York Board of Education for their support of my 1987-1988 Leave of Absence to do ESL research for the elementary level;
- the following people who offered their valuable time and suggestions: Jean Handscombe, Lynn Wilson, Lynn McLean, Pat Watson, Michele Weber, Bob Pletsch, Joan Leslie-Biro, Barb Beckley and Wayne McRoberts, Andy McLachlan and Carina van Heyst, Holly Mina, Lynne Miranda, Mary Reilly, Irwin Silverman, Mariel Danesi, Geof Price, Marian Lydbrooke, Dan DeKuyper, Bernie Dobrowolsky, Shirley Yeung, Al Beattie, Liz Dees, Barb Lichman and Lezlie Litvak.

For easing the load and adding the laughter, major thanks to Pat Treen, Sandy Rosso and Miriam MacPherson, and finally, thanks to Susan Schwartz for sending me to Irwin Publishing.

Introduction

Teaching to Diversity: Teaching and Learning in the Multi-Ethnic Classroom introduces the latest theories about second-language acquisition along with tested teaching approaches and practices for use in elementary schools. It is designed for all educators (not only English-as-a-Second Language teachers) who wish to adapt their repertoire of skills to help recently arrived immigrants, students who were born in Canada and also students for whom a lack of English literacy skills may be delaying their learning in regular classrooms.

Many urban and outlying boards of education expect increasing amounts of diversity among their student clientele in the years to come; for example,

• diversity of cultures and languages,

and

• diversity in proficiencies of student academic skills.

Classroom teachers face the challenges this diversity presents to traditional programming with varying levels of comfort. Many teachers feel they have inadequate knowledge of which skills they should develop in order to program successfully in a culturally and linguistically diverse environment.

Professional material on second-language acquisition and teaching has tended to be geared towards those teachers specifically interested in specializing in English as a Second Language (ESL) and such materials have generally included a rather extensive research and/or linguistic component.

Teaching to Diversity, on the other hand, synthesizes current information on second-language issues in a form that is eminently practical and usable by the regular classroom teacher as well as by the ESL teacher. It is also directly applicable to professional development.

The material in *Teaching to Diversity* draws from, and ties in, research on both first- and second-language acquisition. Hence, it will become clear throughout the book that good second-language teaching practices will benefit all students in our classrooms.

The initial chapters share important background information on key aspects of second-language acquisition. Subsequently, practical aspects of programming for diversity will be shared in chapters on Active Learning, Integrated Language Learning, Cooperative Learning and Education for a Global Perspective.

As a teacher-trainer, my many years in both ESL and regular grade assignments have helped me to understand the connections between theory and practice in teaching. I have grown to be as much a teacher advocate as a child advocate. I am also convinced that working with ESL students is a realm of teaching that will give you, as it has me, a lot of immediate and positive feedback, often much more so than in regular teaching. You see gains so rapidly.

You rejoice in the children's pride in their first spoken words, or in their speed in acquiring reading skills in English ... or in their delight at the first fallen snow!

You smile to yourself at the chatter of loud voices showing there really is more to these newcomers than the quiet, timid façade you initially saw. You will be enriched by your contacts with peoples of other cultures, from the students themselves, their parents and myriad stories of different human experiences that will make you re-evaluate your own life and our North American complacency.

As their teacher, you will have a profound influence on ESL students through your sustained, personal interactions with these children. I hope that *Teaching to Diversity* will provide insights and practical suggestions that will help you to create that bond and help you to open the doors to mutual understanding and success.

Mary Meyers
Spring 1993

If I can ease one heart the pain
I won't have lived in vain.

Elizabeth Barrett Browning

1

Immigrant Children and Language Acquisition

I mmigrant children enter our classrooms from the four corners of the globe: from desperate flights of freedom or on pampered first-class air flights; from shacks in a refugee holding camp or from expensive homes in a modern city; from the country of their birth or from their fourth country of transit. Students may come with both parents or with a sole parent, usually the mother, or with the family of a fortunate relative. Your new student may have come from a strong educational system, know how to read and write fluently in the native language and possess mathematical skills that may surpass the current North American grade level norms. On the other hand, your new student may have missed years of schooling in the native tongue. That same child, however, may speak six languages fluently, or four, or one. In many cases, children of immigrant parents are born in this country yet enter school not speaking English. The immigrant child that you greet today may have left behind a secure and happy life with treasured friends, or perhaps—nightmarish experiences of hunger, separation, fear and death.

How are we teachers to make sense of these crucial factors that affect both *the rate and the amount of English language skills that an English-as-a-Second-Language (ESL) student learns?*

In order to better understand and plan for an ESL learner's needs, it is important to gather pertinent information about that student's background experiences. In effect, what we are doing is building up a profile of that student's educational or learning variables. Blackline Master #4 is a Sample Background Information Sheet for a Newly Arriving ESL Student; Figure 9.2, on page 85, shows the form as it might look when filled out.

It is usually possible to get this information on the same day as the family registers the child, because the family is often accompanied by a trusted translator. Otherwise, plan for a parent conference as soon as possible to examine some background issues for the new student. If a student was born here, or arrived several years ago, inquire about the background from the previous teacher(s).

Figure 1.1 displays some general headings that can be used to guide your initial inquiries about a new student. Factors in each of these areas may affect the rate of that child's learning and for this reason, each heading will be discussed further.

Figure 1.1

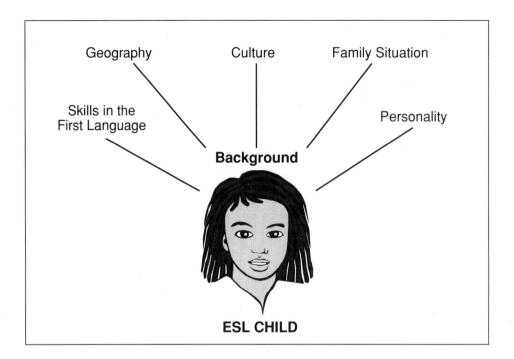

Geography

A colleague once related this saying: "War is the devil's way of teaching geography." While refugees are not the main source of immigration to North America, they certainly make up the group about whom we teachers may have the greatest concern. Refugees, in the main, have chosen to come to our shores because they *must* leave their homeland. War and concern for personal safety do not leave people with many choices for their future or for that of their families.

The emotional baggage that refugees bring may have disrupting consequences for many years after their arrival in the new land. Although we may never be able to comprehend what some families have endured, it is important for us as teachers to learn as much as possible about incoming students. Living in special refugee holding camps or living in transit in various countries is often part of their recent and past experiences. While such experiences most certainly affect the entire family's sense of security, they also have an impact on the educational foundations and futures of the children.

Your students may include children of highly educated people who have missed years of schooling, and *that disadvantage must not be held against them.* In fact, with **adequate** training in basic literacy and upgrading, these students usually make incredible gains in English academic skills. Students of illiterate parents can make similar gains as well. *There is no justification for prejudging immigrant students because of their lack of previous schooling.*

Before you meet with parents, seek out information that explains issues related to the immigration of your newly arriving students. In this way, you will talk with families from a position of some knowledge and empathy instead of unawareness. Locate the countries of origin of your new students. See where they are in relation to countries you know. What are the bordering countries and what are the politics or civil strife in that region of the world? Consult that ethnic group's community associations, consulate or local newspaper for information. Often boards of education will have staff who can provide multicultural background information.

Figure 1.2

The Phothirath family fled to Canada eleven years ago. The new Communist government in Laos had sent the entire family to a re-education camp in the jungle to "rehabilitate" the father, a former Laotian colonel. During their first year in Canada, the children did not go to the ESL summer school program because their grandparents were coming from France to teach them French. The children are all high achievers and well adjusted. The parents, who had been middle-class, educated professionals in their native land, now work long hours at menial jobs.

Figure 1.3

Gon and Hyuk are from Korea. Their father is general manager of an international shipping company and the family will be returning to Korea next year. The boys had very good first-language skills in literacy and mathematics. Hyuk had studied English before, so he could read and write basic English. However, he was not comfortable with the speed at which Canadians spoke English and he certainly didn't have the confidence or previous oral practice necessary for verbalizing in English. Gon had no previous exposure to English. A Canadian employee in their father's company was able to assist the family with school registration, ESL classes for the mother and many other cultural issues that surfaced.

Culture

As you find out a little information about a country, you will become aware of the culture as well. Language and culture are closely related. While it is not expected that we teachers will become highly knowledgeable about every culture represented in our classrooms, it is helpful for us to know the name of the language(s) the children speak and whether their written script is different from our Roman script. Many ESL students have learned a different language in their previous school than was spoken in their homes; so English could be their third or fourth language. It is also very helpful to know that many people have an intolerance for milk before you teach the standard North American food guides or to know that Muslim observance of fasting during Ramadan may affect those students who have had no food since dawn.

You can also learn about your students' special days, religions and cultures by encouraging ESL students' contributions during class discussions. The more information sharing that goes on, the more students will become part of, and not be outside of, your ongoing curriculum.

Being sensitive to those areas in our own culture that will seem new and bizarre to many of your new ESL students will allow you to see our own customs anew. How will you explain the jolly, fat man in the red suit that makes children so excited every December? Many of us have heard the story about the Vietnamese family who had just got settled in their new home only to be terrorized on that first night (October 31) by masked hooligans who kept up a steady barrage of screaming and knocking on the door.

Family Situation

Many factors fall under this heading, including:

- **Are the parents alive and are they together with the children?**
  I have had students from Hong Kong with an absent parent, as well as children from war-torn countries whose parent(s) have been killed, imprisoned or are missing.
- **Are or have the siblings been separated? How long and where?**
  Often, one child is given over to a trusted relative who is ready to immigrate. In other cases, an older sibling has come ahead and paved the way for the rest of the family. Sometimes, it takes years before the whole family can be reunited.
- **Have all the siblings had schooling? In which languages?**
  Many older students have had some training in English in their homeland. They may read and write basic English but they do not understand the rapid pace of our speech or they haven't had much experience verbalizing in English. Their younger siblings, however, may not even know our alphabet system. Moreover, students who have lived in several countries often have learned to read and write in a language that is different from the language(s) spoken in their homes.
- **Has the family joined friends or relatives in the new country?**
  A family is fortunate if it lives or associates with someone who can assist with translations, services and generally explain our customs. Such assistance helps to reduce the impact of culture shock that all immigrants experience.
- **What is the family's immigration status?**
  A refugee is initially not allowed to work in this country and that may give you some indication of the family's financial status. This information is especially important to remember if there are several children within that family who may be asked for trip monies. Also, the students will be absent from school off and on when their immigration hearings occur.
- **Is there someone in the home who can speak any English?**
  If a student is highly motivated and there is someone in the home who can assist with homework, then language acquisition can be speeded up. It is also important to know if school notes or notices will be understood by anyone in the home.
- **Is anyone in the household employed?**
  The D. family from Egypt had seven children. The older two went to work to support their mom and siblings. They spoke little English and did not get a chance to learn English on the job. The younger children, however, acquired English rapidly and became the family translators. During the first winter when the children's clothes were inadequate, the ESL teacher introduced the family to the local Red Cross association for emergencies.

Figure 1.4

This little boy has only been in Canada for a month. His lost look is typical of recent arrivals. That look really says, "I'm not comfortable or confident or sure of what's going on. I don't know what to expect and I really don't think I like this. I'm on overload." Basically —it's culture shock. He needs some hooks to grab on to— like a friend and lots of smiles.

Figure 1.5

Mrs. Abdi came to Canada from Somalia with eight children. Her husband was killed in the war. Five children in the Abdi family came to register at their new elementary school. In their homeland, Farida and Habon had attended a school where they had learned to speak, read and write French. Their home language is Somali. When the civil war started, the younger three children didn't go to school. When the family came to Canada, Said, who had no previous schooling, was placed age appropriately in a Grade 3 with intensive ESL language and literacy support.

Figure 1.6

Aryan and Anahita were very happy to find many other Farsi speakers in their new school. Their mother had completed a Doctorate from a major US university when she was younger. She was, therefore, able to help the children bridge the gap between their native language (Farsi) and English and their Iranian culture and the new Canadian culture.

- **Does the family have knowledge of its ethnic associations in our city?** Knowing where to turn for assistance and advice is essential for all of us, and is even more so for a new immigrant family with few cultural connections to this new country.
- **Has the child witnessed or been the victim of any trauma before or during the move to our country?** At the end of this chapter is a moving story written by a young girl about her experiences in Guatemala before she and her family came to Canada.
- **Is the family here for business, for example, for a three-year term?** The motivation to learn to communicate in a new language may not be as great if children think they will be "going home" again soon.
- **Has a parent or family member had previous experience with North American culture?** For example, attended a university in Canada or the United States.

Skills in the First Language

Children who know how to read and write in their first language will learn to read and write English quickly because their familiarity with literacy will transfer to the learning of English literacy skills.

Students who can do multiplication and division in their native language do not need to be taught those concepts all over again. What they do need to know are the English words that label their existing knowledge.

A student's previous experience or lack of experience with schools will affect the speed of his or her English skills acquisition. Students transfer not only their first-language skills in literacy but

- **their perceptions of themselves as learners,**
- **their coping strategies for how to learn,**

and

- **their skills at socializing.**

Therefore, it is a much easier task for ESL students to adjust to the new school expectations when *they already have a good idea of the purposes and means to learn in one language*. Conversely, it can be a little overwhelming for both the ESL student and the teacher when there is little previous exposure to institutional learning, expectations, and routines, and the child is faced with *the double task of learning both language and literacy basics*.

It is essential that students in this category receive the necessary support in both areas.

Personality

Children's self-esteem, pride in their own talents or skills, intrinsic and extrinsic motivation (parental expectations), health, stability and security within the family—all of these factors will affect the students' desire and ability to socialize and learn at school.

Figure 1.7

A group of mutually supportive Farsi speakers all originally from Iran. Milad, right foreground, spoke Farsi as his first language. His family had lived in Spain before coming to Canada, so Milad spoke Spanish as his second language. Although Farsi was his dominant language, all of his previous literacy education was in Spanish. Spanish and English have a similar alphabet and phonetic base, so Milad had this advantage in starting English reading and writing skills.

A child who is not normally timid and who has a strong interpersonal learning style will create for himself or herself *the best condition for language learning—that of a supportive, interactive group of peers.*

In a case like this, the child actively seeks out friends, joins a group even if he/she can't yet grasp the language demands, and assertively becomes involved with play and lesson situations. Omar in Figure 1.8 was one such student. Layan was another (Figure 1.9).

All ESL students will acquire a speaking vocabulary in English but at different speeds. Just as everybody learns to speak in their first language regardless of their intelligence or personal learning styles, so it is with learning a second language. Insecure students will need nurturing in order to develop their learning potential, so that they will become greater risk-takers, become more involved and be more assured of their right to interact within the social and academic spheres.

Figure 1.8

Omar was disadvantaged in several ways. He had never been to school before being placed age appropriately in Grade 2. He had been separated from his mother for three years and he had witnessed a murder during the civil war in Somalia. But Omar was fortunate in other ways. His mother had been living in Canada and going to school so she knew English and our culture well enough to help Omar over the culture shock. She expected and motivated Omar to learn. Probably the most important factor of all, though, to influence the rate of Omar's learning was his personality—his strengths in the areas of interpersonal skills. He is outgoing and a risk-taker, and was keen to talk even when he was still at a basic level of speaking English.

Figure 1.9

Smiling Layan's older sisters had been sent elsewhere with relatives to avoid the civil war in Somalia and for their schooling. They spoke and read and wrote in French fluently. But Layan (centre) had never been to school before her placement in a Grade 3 class. So she was at a great disadvantage. You can tell by looking at her, though, that Layan doesn't seem to be shy, retiring or even aware of any disadvantage. That's because after six to eight months Layan had focused her considerable talents to learn both to read and write English as easily as she acquired a speaking vocabulary. Layan is an outgoing, sociable risk-taker and this inclination to interact and become involved with all opportunities for language-learning has speeded up her rate of language and literacy acquisition. It was a great boon that her older siblings were able to offer assistance at home with the homework we sent. ***If I know that a student will do homework and that he/she has an English resource at home, then we embark on a homework plan to speed up the learning.***

Some ideas you might try:

- Assign a buddy who speaks the same language and can translate assignments, coming events and routines.
- When you indicate warmth, friendliness and a willingness to communicate and meet with parents, you will always have an ally.
- Have a pep talk with the class to encourage the children to take the new student under their wing. Students will suggest many ways they will help.
- Try to find a particular area of strength and build class awareness of that strength, e.g., art, humour, expertise in first-language stories, sociability, progress, travel in other countries, etc.
- Seek out a recess and lunchtime playmate, if need be from another class.
- Put the child in situations with a really friendly, garrulous student.
- Provide for supportive, risk-free, friendly, interactive class dynamics.

Chapter 9, "What To Do When They Arrive Brand New," and Blackline Masters #1, #2, and #3, "Classroom Teacher's List of Strategies That Enhance Second-Language Acquisition: Atmosphere (#1), Program (#2), and Interaction (#3)," provide many more suggestions to help you involve your ESL students in your daily curriculum.

EQUITY AND REDRESS FOR REFUGEE ESL STUDENTS

Non-English speaking students have generally received special language skills training on a scheduled withdrawal basis within each school. ESL students who are refugees and/or who have missed years of schooling, however, may continue to require intensive literacy—and often, emotional—support long after they have acquired spoken English. Unfortunately, some school boards and administrators do not yet allow for the unique literacy needs of traumatized refugee students or for the social/emotional adjustment needs of those students and their families. They make no differentiation between regular immigrants and those classed as refugees.

It is essential that school policy-makers and administrators ensure adequately trained staff who will be able to provide appropriate language and literacy programs for beginning level refugee ESL students. It is also vital that these policy-makers and administrators provide suitable "reception" programs for new refugee families.

"The involvement of service providers in the post-trauma lives of child survivors *can contribute to the rebuilding process or may inadvertently revictimize [children]*....Appropriate, sensitive and supportive service delivery requires from providers a commitment to learn about refugees, their experiences and their cultures as well as [a] willingness to be creative and flexible in the service approach." (De Monchy 1991; italics mine)

In addition to language and literacy training, a suitable program for refugee students will allot time and attention to:

- family reception and orientation;
- issues of resettlement and inter-agency collaboration;
- use of bilingual support/tutoring;

and

> • guidance provision for mental health and family adjustment needs.
>
> Policy-makers and administrators who fail to provide such redress for the plight and conditions of refugee families or who are unaware or unsympathetic to educational interventions that may be required to meet the unique needs of refugees are essentially *perpetuating a system of inequity*. The failure of schools to address the emotional and family needs of refugee students impedes these children's ability to access further learning and imperils their—and our—futures.
>
> "Unfortunately, arrival to this land of freedom does not in itself fulfill this dream for a bright new future. Rebuilding lives is a long, difficult process exacerbated by the new stresses and traumas of adjustment and acculturation. During resettlement, the legacy of living with terrorism and war is ever-present. Without appropriate support services and interventions, the result will be intense, violent, and costly to the survivors and to society as a whole." (De Monchy 1991)

Summary

Remember that almost all new ESL students go through a **"silent period"** when they hold back to "test the waters." This period may last for many months. In the meanwhile, a friendly, nurturing classroom environment will encourage any child who is anxious, depressed, self-conscious or homesick.

At the end of this chapter are two stories. The first one is about a teacher's lifelong relationship with one of her ESL students; the second is an account of one little girl's memories.

Figure 1.10

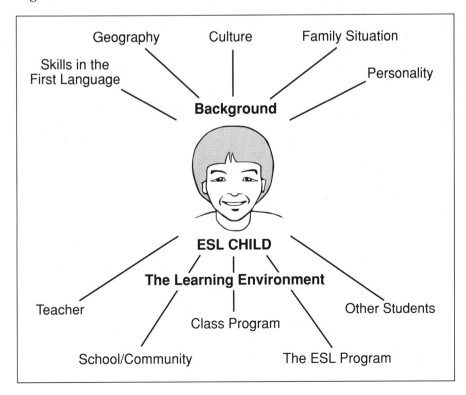

An Addition to Figure 1.1

The original graphic depiction in Figure 1.1 of factors in ESL students' backgrounds that may affect their learning can now be extended to an area that usually lies outside of the children's control—that of the learning environment in which they are placed. These new headings will not be elaborated upon here. However, you may find it useful to consider what thoughts stand out for you under each heading and how each area may have either a positive or a dilatory effect on a new student's adjustment.

A TEACHER'S STORY

In front of me is a photo of two people; one is me, the handsome boy is P. We are both smiling, full from Christmas dinner. P. has his coat on—ready to go meet his girlfriend when she finishes work. After that he will go back to his other home, to the home of his sister—the guardian who took P. at age two when their parents starved to death; back to the sister who dragged him through "the killing fields" of Cambodia to the Thai camps; who finally brought him to Canada—a family member, yes...not beloved, not nurtured...but alive!

P. came into my class when he was eight, we think. His age and birthdate were not really clear in his sister's memory. She had been through so much herself. P. is now eighteen. He has a soft, deep voice and has worn a moustache for a year. P. calls me his stepmother now. I silently chuckled when he first said that. But I was also pleased. My name is proudly on his school registration form as the contact person.

When I first met him, P. was a "runner"—a child who ran from home when the fighting got bad. The neighbours would feed him, we were told, and he would sleep in the apartment stairwells under newspaper. It's funny, though, that he was never absent from school. Once, when P. fell asleep in class, we just worked around him.

With his sister's permission, I started to include P. on family outings and to a relative's cottage for a summer trip. He came for weekends and finally, he came for Easter and for Christmas. I guess any holiday would create some free time for P. to come and stay. He is like an older brother to my son.

Once when P. went missing for three weeks, my son and I looked in the ghetto where he lived and hung out. We searched for him, asking who saw him, leaving our phone number. Whenever we saw any Cambodian teenagers, we'd hop out of the car and ask about P. It seemed a perfectly normal thing to ask because P. is so sociable that almost everybody knew him and I knew that. It was P.'s pattern—stay away from the home as much as possible and make many friends whom you could rely on.

Well, he had slept at several friends' homes for a while and then when we finally caught up with him, he had been sleeping in a cardboard box in back of an apartment. P.'s needs were pretty basic—food and friends. I asked him—"Why didn't you call us?" P. said he forgot the phone number. I believe him. Now he gives a copy of our number to his girlfriend, in case he ever forgets again.

Each year, I phoned the new schools P. attended. I became a P. advocate because he had nobody to watch out for him—and he really needed it. I would confer with the homeform teacher about P. and I would fill in the guidance people on what P. was all about, what program he might be steered towards. But even with my persistence and knowledge of how the system works, P. fell through every single loophole that could exist. You see, although P. learned to speak English faster than any other child I know, he remains to this day, functionally illiterate.

Whether the deprivation of nourishment or love while he was a baby is the cause for his inability to learn to read or write now, we'll never know for sure. What does matter now though, at eighteen years of age, is that he get job training and develop needed life skills, such as how to fill out applications, or how to use the subway. Recently, I enrolled him in a good vocational school and we are looking at some form of co-op work-study program so he can earn money while getting on-the-job training. His dream is to one day be able to pass his driver's test.

P. is a wonderful boy. Despite his incredible past and any present problems, he is honest, optimistic, street smart and drug-free. I know there will be long stretches with P. not around but I consider myself lucky for those many times in the years ahead when he'll be a part of our family.

When I think of teaching P., or any other new immigrant student, I want to know what I'm dealing with—what has the child been through, what is the family situation, what are the native language skills—in short, I want to know all the pluses for that student and all the drawbacks that will affect his/her learning and success in my classroom.

First Memory: Destruction of the World

*By Lucie de Bruin Valerius Fuentes, a refugee from Guatemala. Printed in **The Toronto Star**, Sunday Edition—one of nine stories printed in **The Star** out of more than 400 children's short stories submitted to **The Sunday Star's** short story contest held at the beginning of the summer of 1989. When she wrote this story Lucie de Bruin Valerius Fuentes was in Grade 8.*

When I try to go as far, far, far back as I can, the very first thing that I remember in life is the destruction of the world. Much later, I learned that the date was February 4, 1972, and that it was 3 o'clock in the night. I was almost 4 years old.

It taught me that the earth is not solid and safe the way it seems to us but that we live on something that resembles the broken shell of an egg. We are never safe. Never.

That night, I awoke by being thrown up and down and sideways against the bars around my bed. There was a tremendously loud roaring sound. Furniture toppled, the TV set fell on the floor, large paintings fell from the wall. The loudest noise came from the kitchen. Pots and pans were thrown against the walls and the floor. Pottery shattered. Even the huge fridge fell against the door, which splintered. The glass of the windows broke.

For a moment, the lights came on. But then they went out again and we stayed in pitchdark.

My mom pulled me up from bed by my hair. I heard dad shouting, "Where is Lucie? She is not in her bed." My mom answered, "Run, I have Lucie."

I see myself in my memory being held by my hair and carried out of the house. But since you cannot see yourself being carried as from a distance, even when it isn't dark, it must be that I have heard my mom tell the story so often that it became like memory.

Everything was breaking apart and falling down. When my mother put me down in the garden where she had run, we both fell. The ground was rocking up and down...

Then, all at once, everything was still and silent. My mother started to cry and to pray. We thought that it was over.

But the earth started to rock again, although not as violently as before. We heard dogs bark and people cry out in the dark. Weird sounds came from deep beneath the ground.

At daybreak, we wanted to

leave but could do so only by going through the house and out of the front door. The house could collapse at any moment, so my dad held me in his arms and ran as fast as he could to the door. But it stuck and he had to put me down and get an axe to open it. Then my mom ran out but some waterpipe had burst and everything flooded. She fell and had to be helped out.

Outside, people were crying and groaning. Others prayed loudly together. Later I learned that this had been an earthquake and that 24,000 people had died during the first shock.

You cannot trust the earth you live on. It is treacherous. Disaster and death can strike at any moment, even while you are fast asleep.

The archbishop said that it was a punishment of God. I cannot believe that God commits massacres like the soldiers of our country.

My father wanted to drive to the coast, where he said that we would be safe. Everywhere we passed we saw ruins. We came to a village that had completely fallen in ruins; not one single house still stood. The Indians had dug huge holes and they threw heaps of bodies into them.

Sometimes roads were closed because of landslides, ruins or rubble and then dad had to drive back and take dirt paths. At long last, we reached the ocean. There we stayed for two months in a hotel near the beach.

*   *   *

I don't remember much of my early life afterwards, except that I was happy and had a lot of fun. I do not know how, why or when all this changed.

Like on a hot and sunny day, when you lie with your eyes closed lazily in the grass.

Then all at once you feel a chilly shadow over you. Opening your eyes, the blue sky is gone. Instead, a black thundercloud has come between you and the sun. At the same time a cold and wet wind has sprung up. The thunder and rain can come at any moment.

It started when something happened to the father of my best friend. The real bad thing was that there was some dreadful secret. Even my friend didn't really know what had happened to her own father. Something horrible had occurred and we knew that he was dead. We just knew it. What made it worse was that we couldn't talk about it or ask questions. It was one of those things grownups don't explain to kids.

Don Pancho was next. He was a neighbor. He was old and grumpy and none of us kids liked him. Then one day he just wasn't there. Everybody did as if he had never existed. As if nothing had happened. That was scary.

I'll never forget the day that my best friend, who's dad had disappeared, didn't come to school

any more. I asked the teacher why but she got awfully mad at me and beat me and told me not ever to ask such stupid questions again.

I remember how mom cried when an uncle died. I had been listening behind the door and had heard that he had been shot in a street. I still don't know who he was. Mom has a very big family.

*   *   *

The very worst part was the secret behind the disappearance and death of all those people we knew. All us kids knew that there was danger. That we could be next. Anytime any of us could just be killed, just like in the earthquake. But you couldn't ask anyone. Just like sex, it was a forbidden subject. We could only whisper all kinds of horror stories to each other.

At home, things were wrong too. I once saw that my father had a pistol in his pocket. He once showed me a spray-can and told me that if anybody would enter the house with force to spray him with it. He would then drop down for 10 minutes. Meanwhile I and mom could run to grandmother's house.

Once, soldiers stormed into our house during the night. But nothing happened. At first they shouted and cursed. But my father laughed with them and told jokes. He gave them lots of rum to drink and money and they just left. My mom and I had been hiding in a closet.

Kids were being picked up by the police and soldiers and were never heard from again, so I didn't go to school any longer. We were not allowed to play outside anymore and had to stay home or in the garden.

*   *   *

All at once life changed completely. One day I was in a plane and we came to Canada.

How happy I felt to walk in the wide, clean avenues of Toronto. How happy I was to live without fear.

I bite my nails all the time. I am afraid to be alone, my dad says that I grind my teeth in my sleep. It seems that the fear has not entirely gone but has gone into hiding. Maybe it's like you have washed your dirty hands but afterwards still find some dirt behind your nails.

Within three months, I became a Canadian citizen. But I really felt a Canadian kid when I had earned it and had learned to speak English. All day long until bedtime I studied lists of words and within six months I spoke English. How proud I felt!

My next task is to go to university later and to become a doctor.

My first memory is not to take the earth for granted. Earthquakes don't happen here, but an A-bomb could flatten Toronto, the air and water can become polluted, the ozone layer can be damaged. We should do everything we can to prevent this.

My last memories in Guatemala were that you cannot trust people. Well, Canada is not ruled by police or soldiers and we should make certain that it will never happen. Canada is ruled by businessmen. Their creed is money. We should be careful that they won't corrupt the government and that it is ruled for the benefit of all of us.

Yes, I know, kids shouldn't tell grownups what to do. But we kids are not dumb and I hope that the dreadful nightmares I have lived through may build some understanding about life.

Sometimes I feel much older than my classmates.

2 First Languages: Help or Hindrance?

Generally, teachers are surprised at how quickly and easily ESL students acquire the spoken English language. Current research, however, states that it takes many years to acquire English fluency in the areas of **both speech** *and* **literacy**. In the face of this research, it becomes essential that effective approaches be identified and developed to advance quality programs during the length of time it takes students to develop full English proficiency.

In subsequent chapters of *Teaching to Diversity*, I will outline and discuss the merits of several approaches to ensure the best possible programs in multi-ethnic classrooms. In this chapter, I will outline rudimentary strategies and also provide compelling reasons not only to rely on the strengths of a student's native language but actively to promote the maintenance and development of those first-language skills.

In "Bilingualism Without Tears," Merrill Swain presents principles that are "crucial to second-language development, academic success and emotional well-being."

> **The first principle, that of first things first, establishes the central role of the child's first language in all aspects of his or her educational development....To be told, whether directly or indirectly, explicitly or implicitly, that your language and the language of your parents, of your home and of your friends is non-functional in school is to negate your sense of self...the first language is so instrumental to the emotional and academic well-being of the children, that its development must be seen as a high, if not the highest, priority in the early years of schooling.**

Allowing children to use their native languages in class— for example, to translate for newcomers, to discuss new ideas or tasks, to share their languages on bulletin boards or on notes home to parents—serves to affirm the students' languages and cultures and to bolster self-esteem.

GOOD NEWS!
There is a growing body of consistent and convincing evidence that the development, retention and use of a child's native language will also benefit their English skill development in the areas of cognition and literacy. **See, for example: Cummins (1986, 1984, 1983, 1981), Cummins and Swain (1986), Swain (1983), Di Giovanni and Danesi (1988), Early (1990), Samuda (1986), Wells (1987, 1986), Chamot (1983), Derman-Sparks (1989), Ambert (1988), Enright and McCloskey (1988, 1985), Saville-Troike (1985), McLaughlin (1985, 1984), Meyers (1988).**

Jim Cummins (1984) of the Modern Languages Centre at the Ontario Institute for Studies in Education (OISE) in Toronto points out that the kinds of English that students use during face-to-face and day-to-day conversations is a far cry from the types of language proficiency that are ultimately required in academic and textbook assignments.

It is now generally accepted that *within two years* most ESL students develop sufficient English proficiency to handle day-to-day school and peer social situations. This type of language tends to be related to personal matters, real objects and present events, in short, to the daily life of the child.

However, this two-year span also refers mainly to the development of oral language and herein lies a problem. Some children seem to *speak* English so well and so soon that it comes as an unpleasant surprise when not all their English skills are as well developed. Have you ever thought or heard this?

"He speaks English fine but his reading and writing are really weak."

"Why isn't she making better progress in reading or writing? Maybe, she isn't as smart as I thought she was."

Although an ESL student may appear to converse well in everyday class situations, that child often still lacks the "fluency, accuracy and range of language" of a native English speaker.
—North York Board of Education (1988)

The real problem for second-language learners is the language used in academic subjects and, especially, in textbooks. It is this type of English proficiency and demands for vocabulary comprehension that can take five to nine years to develop. The language used in specialty subjects and textbooks tends to be rather formal and slightly abstract, with new and specific terminology for concepts in each subject. *In short, this type of language is substantially different from the English we use in everyday spoken interactions and it is, therefore, not only a lot more difficult to understand, it is also much more challenging for ESL students to carry over and produce that language in their written assignments or "to use" during discussions.* For a broader understanding of the types of language skills students need to acquire to be truly proficient in English, see Figure 2.1. Chapter 3, "Language Teaching and Learning," also discusses this issue of what really constitutes proficiency.

The criteria for evaluating an ESL student's English ability has tended to be on the basis of that student's skills in social or spoken language. The ESL student who appears to speak and understand everyday basic communication is usually expected to function just as successfully with the diverse language demands of a regular classroom, including literacy—with no further language

Figure 2.1

Number of Years Required To Achieve Native-like English Proficiency

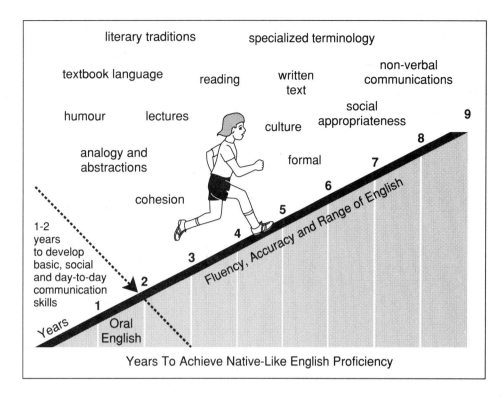

literary traditions   specialized terminology

textbook language   reading   written text   non-verbal communications

humour   lectures   culture   social appropriateness   9

analogy and abstractions   formal   8

cohesion   7

Fluency, Accuracy and Range of English

6

5

4

3

2

1-2 years to develop basic, social and day-to-day communication skills

1

Years   Oral English

Years To Achieve Native-Like English Proficiency

support or modifications deemed necessary. Future problems may then be attributed to that ESL child's lack of ability rather than to inappropriate policies, programs and teaching strategies.

It is unreasonable to expect second-language learners to reach their potentials or to function as successfully as native English speakers in a regular classroom program with no modifications in the presentation of concepts and related assignments. *This idea of the longer time-frame that ESL students need to achieve native-like fluency in language skills and literacy skills is one that many educators have not come to realize or understand* (Meyers 1988).

Implications of this longer time-frame for classroom teachers include the following.

• **Logistically, it is not feasible for ESL students to receive special, withdrawal, ESL support for the five to nine years it may take to reach native-like proficiency in academic language skills.**
• **There will, therefore, be ESL students in classes who need modifications in the presentation and delivery of new curricular concepts.**
• **It becomes essential to incorporate teaching approaches and strategies that enable both students and teachers to meet success in the interim.**
• **Standardized tests may not reflect the actual cognitive strengths and abilities of our second-language learners; because the students may not understand the test type language, their responses may not accurately reflect their ability. Therefore, the best assessment procedures for ESL students include methods that ensure measurement of student comprehension as well as indicating skills developed. (See also Blackline Masters #1, #2, and #3, "Classroom Teacher's List of Strategies That Enhance Second-Language Acquisition: Atmosphere (#1), Program (#2), and Interaction (#3).")**

The Development and Retention of First-Language Skills

The concept of human dignity is fundamentally linked to the life of the mind which in turn is closely linked to language as a basic form of communication. Language is a rudiment of consciousness and close to the core of personality; deprivations in relation to language deeply affect personality....
                                    —McDougall, Laswell and Chen in Ashworth (1985)

Once, not so long ago, it was thought that ESL students should speak only English during the school day. Not only that, but many educators urged their students' parents to speak English at home too.

In *Hunger of Memory*, Richard Rodriguez describes the devastating effect on his family life, of teachers' advice to his parents that he and his siblings speak English at home. Because his parents spoke only limited English, conversations became fewer and fewer and misunderstandings abounded. Both his parents and the children grew frustrated and eventually all that was heard around the dinner table was the "clinking of knives and forks against dishes."

In direct contrast is the story Leo Buscaglia, internationally known author and lecturer, who tells of his family dinners during which everyone spoke Italian, their first language. For him, dinner was a time of conviviality, building family bonds and intellectual striving as his father expected each of his children to tell of one thing that they had learned that day. Buscaglia makes us laugh along with him as he challenges us to imagine the fast thinking skills he developed whenever he was unable to remember anything and it was getting closer to his turn.

Buscaglia's story echoes a belief in the advantages that children have in acquiring skills at school if the parents have involved them in discussions and decision making that require them to think things through in the home language.

Concomitant with current research on minority student education, two classroom strategies can now be stated:
- **build children's self-esteem and confidence regarding their heritage, language, culture and abilities—you will empower them;**
- **use and build on the strengths a child already has in the first language, e.g., cognition, literacy, social skills, special talents.**

Building on the Strengths of the First Language

The very good news about relying on a student's strengths in his or her first language is that skills developed in one language transfer easily and naturally to reflect similar performance in a subsequent language.

In "Empowering Minority Students: A Framework for Intervention," Cummins refers to the fact that language skills and knowledge are transferable from one language to another. For example, a student who has previously learned

Figure 2.2

The important point here is that a student who has well-developed thinking skills (cognition) in his or her first language is probably going to meet more success in school than a student whose first-language development is neglected or minimal. Therefore, encourage parents to extend their interactions with their children in their home language. Just as you advise English-speaking parents who ask how they can help their children at home, counsel parents (who speak a language other than English) to actively include the child during language opportunities such as family discussions, plans, trips and daily reading experiences.

Figure 2.3

From "Bilingualism in the Home," by Jim Cummins, **Heritage Language Bulletin,** *Vol.1, No.1, p.10. Reproduced with permission of the author.*

how to divide, does not have to relearn that skill all over again—he or she just needs to learn the English labels (vocabulary) for those known concepts.

A study from British Columbia concludes that both a student's *first-language competence and the use of that language as a learning resource contributes to academic success* (Early et al 1989). In "What Really Matters in Second Language Learning for Academic Achievement?", researcher Saville-Troike reported that most of the children who achieved best in content areas (measured by tests in English) were those who had had the opportunity to discuss the new concepts in their native language. She concluded that this reliance on and use of children's first languages clearly provided the best context for developing new concepts and for acquiring English.

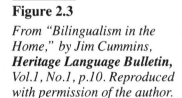

One wheel (one language) can get you places...

So can a big wheel and a little wheel...

However, when your wheels are nicely balanced and fully inflated you'll go further...

Provided, of course, the people who made the wheels knew what they were doing...

A TEACHER SPEAKS

I was at a loss. Here I was with a new student from Vietnam and no translator. Normally, I rely so much on my other students who speak the same languages. Or sometimes I have to get a student from another class to help but this (situation) was really hard on both of us. Finally, I located two younger students whose first language was Vietnamese. Great! However, much to my dismay, neither of these two students would translate in their language. I tried everything: you know. . . rephrasing, simplifying my requests but the little guys (Grade 2) wouldn't translate. Oh, I could see that they were trying. They would turn to each other, whisper in quiet, tiny voices but eventually they stood in troubled silence with the new child. I thanked them and let them go.

In my mind's eye, I can still see them walking down the hall, trying to figure out what they could have said. I've thought about that a lot since. Were they so conditioned not to use their first language in our school setting that they lost their ability and confidence to even talk? They had turned their little faces in and whispered so as to not offend or maybe to hide their language. Surely to God these two could communicate at home with their own families in the first language. Well then, what happened here at school to create this inability to talk, this fear or timidity, whatever? And, then I thought—what was I doing right in my own class that everybody so naturally spoke out and we learned in all our languages?

—M. Patrone, Teacher

In "Empowering Minority Students," Cummins describes educational approaches as being either empowering or disabling, and as either additive or subtractive of culture and language. He argues that if educators see their role as one of replacing or subtracting the students' language and culture so that they can superimpose English, then they are likely to disempower those children. On the other hand, *allowing children to use their first language while they learn is a way to empower students.*

To empower is to enable those who have been silenced to speak.
—Simon (1987)

What Else Can We Do To Empower Students?

- Allow the students to talk in their first languages at activities and during tasks. If the assignment product, that is, the end result, is to be in English, then students may need to talk it through and plan in their first languages. If it is the process that you want the children to do in English, then plan specifically for heterogeneous (mixed) groups or partners.
- Encourage students to translate for one another and for you.
- Have new students write in the language in which they are literate. Have the students show or read their work to the whole class. Perhaps another student could translate. Post both the first- and the second-language versions.

Figure 2.4

(Left) It is important for administrators, whenever possible, to choose staff who reflect the diversity within their schools. (Right) A teacher from Somalia had been hired to teach Somali refugee children who have never had the opportunity to go to school because of civil war in their country. Here, he is working, in Somali, with one of his groups, using place value blocks to upgrade the students' math skills.

- Use translations alongside English for bulletin boards or notes home. Parents will often do these for you if you send home paper and markers.
- Have students translate an overview of new topics or upcoming events.
- Draw attention to bilingual books in your school or public library.
- Actively encourage students to share their views, experiences and cultures during discussions, e.g., special days in the upcoming month.
- Translate important information for parents, e.g., Open House, Parent-Teacher Conferences.
- Invite parents as helpers in class, or on trips. At that time, inquire as to their willingness to act as a resource, e.g., to provide a written background story on the Dragon Boat Race. You will want one copy for yourself in English and another in the first language for display.
- Ask parents to help develop curriculum resource boxes related to their specific cultures. Build collections of sample props from that culture, e.g., photos or posters, art objects, toys, coins, etc.
- Encourage students to plan and deliver a cultural announcement for the rest of the school, e.g., when and how Hindus celebrate the harvest festival of Holi.
- Take photographs of the child's day at school to create a book that the student can take home to show what happens at school. You may want to include photos of routines, new friends, special events, etc.
- Have students compose photo books or posters that will share insights into their family and cultural lifestyles.
- Attend conferences that help promote effective ESL teaching.

Obviously, we teachers cannot be expected to speak, even in a rudimentary way, all the languages of our students. Much of the translation and first-language learning support must come from the ESL students themselves, and awareness of their cultures must be elicited from these same students.

Teachers who establish classroom practices that foster the retention and use of both the students' cultures and languages will be tapping in to their own best resources.

Figure 2.5

"Am I supposed to speak all these languages????"

Chapter 3, "Language Teaching and Learning," will present an overview of language and learning beliefs, in this century, that have affected the shift towards rather dramatic changes in our classroom dynamics.

3 Language Teaching and Learning

Throughout our history, because of exploration, trade, conquest, slavery, migration, interest or, more currently, because of economic interdependence, learning other languages has been part of the human story. As well as providing a brief overview of major theories of language learning prevalent in North America this century, I will discuss the important consequences these theories have had in changing our classroom dynamics— changes that form the basis of the current shift to Active Learning, Integrated Language Learning and Cooperative Learning.

Some Specific Language Learning Methods

1. Grammar Translation Method

This very structured, traditional approach placed a strong emphasis on reading and writing skills. Often, people who had studied a language using this approach still could not speak the language, e.g., Latin or Greek.
Grammar Translation meant:
  • memorizing vocabulary lists and rules (reading),
  • translating literary passages (writing),
  • working through ponderous textbooks (very structured),
and
  • little opportunity to verbalize (almost useless).

2. The Direct Method

The Direct Method represented a total shift away from the study of grammar. There was, instead, a stress on vocabulary that was useful and therefore meaningful. In place of a textbook, visuals, real objects and demonstrations were used in teaching. The Berlitz School of Languages, which opened during this time, still operates successfully today using the Direct Method of teaching languages.

An offshoot of the Direct Method that has left a more lasting impression is the Army Method, more commonly known as the Audio-Lingual Method.

Figure 3.1

The Army Method stressed the ability to speak the language. Soldiers' lives depended on their ability to pass as a native speaker during wartime assignments.

3. The Audio-Lingual Method

The Audio-Lingual Method was developed and funded in response to the US military's needs during the Second World War. During the war, soldiers had to learn to operate in other countries and languages. They had little time to learn to read and write the new language. Their lives depended on their ability to *sound* like native speakers. Although there was some attention to grammar and literacy, the aim was the development of spoken language. Thus, the Audio-Lingual Method focused on listening and speaking skills in a foreign language.

This method was based on B. F. Skinner's research on conditioning. It relied on repetition, pattern drills, structured audio-taped lessons called language labs, visuals, and language skits. Like the Direct Method, the Audio-Lingual Method signified a move away from the very academic and formal approach of Grammar Translation to a belief in the importance of using "real" language versus textbook language.

> **The shift, therefore, was from a traditional linguistic approach to an interactive approach, wherein the language that was taught was meant to be used.**

WHAT WENT WRONG?

Problems arose with the Audio-Lingual Method when it was adopted for use in school language classes.

- The pattern drills, stress on memorization and repetition in lessons were boring for children.
- Student motivation could not equal that of soldiers who were facing a life-and-death situation.

- Soldiers were pre-selected for their aptitude in languages. School language classes, on the other hand, comprised students with mixed abilities.
- The method relied on behaviourist research that viewed language learning in very restrictive terms, because it lacked this insight—*that human cognition and, therefore, language, is infinitely creative.*

Parallel work in the fields of social and human psychology led to an important shift in the approaches favoured for teaching a second language and, as other crucial factors in human learning—cognition, emotions and the contexts of the learning environment—were studied, the Audio-Lingual approach fell into disfavour.

4. Total Physical Response

The Total Physical Response (TPR) Method is particularly effective with children as it places a strong emphasis on learning through physical actions (kinetics). Its methods are similar to action-songs and rhymes that primary classes engage in. There is even a certain reading strategy, called imprinting, that involves following the reading text with a moving finger. Today, mime and gesture are still very much an important strategy to ensure comprehension and language retention with beginning ESL students.

Learning is enhanced by actions that accompany an activity, such as in drama, finger-rhymes, songs, or real experiences. Kinetics (movement) provide a hook to help students remember what they've learned. The use of kinetics has a base in Piaget's maturational stages in cognition (see page 24).

Figure 3.2

Learning Theories

Since the 1950s, there has been a great deal of research into thinking and learning. Several of the theories that have grown out of this research have been instrumental in affecting dramatic changes in educational pedagogy for the last half of the twentieth century. Ausubel's Cognitive Learning Theory, Piaget's maturational stages in cognition, Roger's Humanistic Approach, and finally, Vygotsky's theories on the connections between socialization, language and learning are outstanding examples of such research. Second-language teaching and learning has benefited from this extensive research, as well. In this chapter, you will see how first-language learning theories led naturally to the development of Krashen's Natural Approach in the 1980s and to the most current approach to second-language teaching, Communicative Competence.

The Cognitive Learning Theory

If you believe that comprehension and memory are enhanced when the new material you want to teach is related to or connected with something that students already know or understand, then you are, in essence, a proponent of the Cognitive Learning Theory. The Cognitive Learning Theory, developed in the 1960s largely by David Ausubel, has had long-lasting effects on education. This theory questioned the validity of rote learning and drills, of textbook learning and teacher-centred lessons, of memorization versus meaningful learning. More important, however, Ausubel's work laid the foundations for us as educators

- to develop a better understanding of motivational actors in learning;
- to tie in and show relationships of the present learning to the past experiences and cognitive levels of our students;
- to create learning experiences that would be more meaningful for our students;

and finally,

- to cultivate skills in student-centred teaching and learning.

An example of the Cognitive Learning Theory in action: In the past, many students studied spelling from chapters in a spelling textbook. Currently, however, many teachers derive spelling lists from topics the students are learning (thematic vocabulary) or from the students' own writing errors. In this way, spelling is connected to a real subject and is made meaningful to children.

Developmental Stages of Children's Maturation

The French social scientist Piaget's research into children's learning led him to conclude that there are different levels of maturational readiness for certain skills and cognitive abilities that all children go through. Piaget's work has had a profound influence on education and on our understanding of how, when and what to teach children.

Piaget's research on the different developmental stages of children's thinking and learning implies that schools should allow children to become actively engaged with both manipulative materials and with their peers.

The Humanistic Approach

Carl Rogers' work, like that of Ausubel and Piaget, moved the focus of education away from the teacher and the content of lessons towards the learner and the contexts in which students learn best.

Rogers, an American psychologist working in the 1950s and 1960s, had extensive experience in psychotherapy and research. The impact of Rogers' very humanistic orientation to education has been far reaching. Carl Rogers' work is at the root of many major changes within education. His principles of human behaviour and suggestions for educators opened the way for improving the learning experience for all students.

Rogers advocated:

- an emphasis on developing a risk-taking, anxiety-free atmosphere;
- a shift to Cooperative Learning versus competitive education;
- consideration of individual and socio-cultural variables in learning;
- student-centred, student-initiated learning;
- a rethinking of the teacher's role in the learning process; teachers became facilitators of learning.

A surge of new approaches and techniques in teaching developed from the popularity of Ausubel's and Rogers' ideas. Because the major focus of these new ideas was the needs of the learner, they have been termed Humanistic Methods. The area of second-language learning was also affected.

The Natural Approach

The Natural Approach, introduced in the 1980s (Krashen 1985 and Krashen and Terrell 1983), offered several important additions to our understanding of second-language learning.

- Krashen and Terrell introduced the idea of "comprehensible input," which implies
  – that the child should be able to understand the gist of what is said;
  and
  – that the language used for teaching and interacting with the ESL student should be modified to ensure comprehension.

Language opportunities should be attuned to the learners' levels of fluency.

- The Natural Approach drew similarities between learning a first language and learning a second language. In dealing with non-English speakers, a teacher's speech might sound much like the type of language used by parents with toddlers during first-language acquisition. This kind of language is called "caretaker" speech or "motherese."

  Caretaker speech involves speaking in the here and now, referring to real objects or experiences, emphasizing important content words, and repeating, rephrasing, and expanding the child's speech, where appropriate.

EXAMPLE

Modifications in teacher talk for a non-English speaking student:

> When indicating that it is lunch time and everybody is leaving to eat, the teacher might repeat the words "lunch time—11:30," point to her/his watch, mime eating and make a shooing motion to indicate "out the door." This does not have to be a major dramatic production. However, it may be necessary to repeat this five-second modification several days in a row before simply saying the words,
> "Lunch time, bye. Come back at 12:30."

> More complex language is quickly added as the student indicates that he/she comprehends the original message.

• The Natural Approach recognizes that most beginning students go through a "*silent period*" while they come to grips with routines and expectations, and develop the confidence needed to take risks in language. The length of time of a silent period varies for each child. It may last several months or it could last for as long as a year. The Natural Approach suggests an appropriate atmosphere would accept this phenomenon while at the same time providing encouragement and participation in "meaning-full" language opportunities.

• The Natural Approach views *errors as a natural part of the language-learning process*. Errors in speech should not be corrected unless they seriously affect the meaning of the student's message. In other words, we should never stop the flow of a child's excitement in sharing an idea to correct his or her pronunciation or grammar (unless we don't understand the ideas). We can always make a mental note to address some of these errors at a later time (conferencing/individual feedback).

Showing such restraint is often hard for us as teachers. But, we must try to remember, when students are just beginning to talk they are usually proud of or excited about something and it is most discouraging to be halted, corrected and forced to repeat something. It takes all the fun out of communicating. However, a more advanced ESL student would benefit from *judicial* error-correction in his or her writing, in the same manner as we consider the number and type of errors to remedy with any other student.

Communicative Competence

Communicative Competence describes a broader notion or definition of language proficiency than was previously understood (Hymes, Canale and Swain, and Saville-Troike in McLaughlin 1985). It is necessary to reconsider here just what it is that we expect students will be able to do with the English they learn. What does language proficiency really entail?

The old Grammar Translation Method viewed language proficiency as the knowledge of vocabulary and grammar, but this knowledge did not prepare learners to speak the language.

Any definition of language proficiency has to include the notion of an ability to use the language.

Figure 3.3

The Direct Method and the Audio-Lingual approach stressed the use of oral language, but that wasn't enough. The patterned responses they taught did not take into account the fact that there are an infinite variety of creative ways of saying things and of responding to spoken dialogue. English proficiency means more than an ability to use a set of standard phrases in a given situation.

To be able to communicate successfully, it is also necessary that students *understand* the jargon, slang and social customs of their peers and of our culture—or else they run the risk of being ignored or perhaps worse, of being reviled. Proficiency implies an ability to adjust language to suit the person, group or audience with whom you are talking, to use informal speech with peers and then to use more acceptable forms of address when talking to older people and authority figures.

> **Any definition of language proficiency must include the ability to communicate appropriately with different people in a variety of different social situations.**

COMMUNICATING EFFECTIVELY

The following classroom examples illustrate several competencies that are required in order to communicate effectively in the second language.

1. A peer, at recess, tells the ESL student to, "Come here."
   In class, that ESL child turns to you and says, "Come here."
   Which competency is missing?
2. As a special little duty, you've instructed an ESL student to obtain something from someone, e.g., Ms. Johnson's one-hole punch.
   To check that he understands what's to be done, you ask,
   "What are you going to say?"

The child tries out several versions of a request—all of which seem inadequate and even rather abrupt. You thought his English proficiency was much better than is obviously the case.

What competency is missing?

3. In her oral storytelling and writing, the ESL child does this:
...and...and...and...and...and

What competency is missing?

4. In a group discussion task with peers, an ESL child doesn't seem to get involved or to say much.

What competency is missing?

5. As you were about to begin to conference at her desk, your usually extremely polite ESL student just gave another student "the finger."

What competency is missing?

6. Even though he's a good student, Amin, nevertheless, copies everything verbatim from texts for his written project work. During his oral presentation, Amin reads directly from his report. When asked to tell about it, not to read it, Amin jokes around and spoils his mark.

What competency is missing?

7. Tasmeen is really clever and she has made fabulous progress in such a short time. You can't understand why she did so poorly on the standardized grade tests.

What competency is missing?

WHAT LANGUAGE COMPETENCIES ARE NEEDED?

Example 1. The child is not aware of the use of *register*. In other words, the child is not aware of the correct tones and language suitable to addressing an adult or someone in a position of authority. Inform the child gently that his/her manner of speaking to you was inappropriate, that talking to a child is different from talking to a teacher, and model a more suitable form of calling for attention.

Example 2. The child is missing a *range* of language forms that express questions. He is not familiar with forming more than a basic question. Perhaps during the tension of having to perform a new role, he also forgets to use forms of *politeness*, as well. In all likelihood, he may be using a form that is too *informal* and, therefore, inappropriate towards an adult authority figure. This is a good example of an ESL child carrying over peer-suited speech into other social situations where it is not acceptable. Try several whole-class exercises that involve working together to develop and conduct appropriate questionnaires for various contexts, e.g., students group together to develop a questionnaire to learn more about the principal or a guest speaker (or for a fan letter).

Example 3. The student is unaware of alternative words in English that link one idea with another. The correct term is **cohesion**. This child would benefit from a group lesson that elicits new joining words. Chart and post joining words for students' future reference.

Although the child in **Example 4** is sociable and even understands the group task, he does not have the necessary language "know how" to jump into the conversation, to get a turn, or "hold the floor." The speed of the language flow or turn-taking may also be posing a problem. This is called *strategic competence*.

ESL students need lots of practice in small group talk activities. Also try a teacher-directed lesson that allows you to model conversation strategies at a more leisurely pace.

The student in **Example 5** is learning the emphatic use of non-verbal behaviours in English. Unfortunately, that child lacked prior knowledge of our culture's restrictions on their use. Be straightforward and inform that student of cultural norms when needed.

Example 6. Amin may be a clever boy, but he doesn't yet have the fluency required to paraphrase textbook language. He is not as advanced in his acquisition of English as the teacher assumes. He has not yet developed the *fluency*, *accuracy* and *range* of English of his peers. There are several skills involved here: the ability to understand the specialized vocabulary of a densely written text and the ability to express an idea in alternate ways.

Indeed, most native English speakers need help with these particular skills as well. You could elicit class ideas on good public speaking-presentation style.

Amin also needs lots of practice with reporting and evaluating similar tasks in smaller groups.

Example 7. Tasmeen does speak English well in social situations, but she is not yet as capable with the types of language used in written discourse and test-type language. It takes time and familiarity with similar test tasks to develop these skills. Remember, *written language differs significantly in many ways from spoken language*.

Figure 3.4

Language proficiencies that together make up Communicative Competence

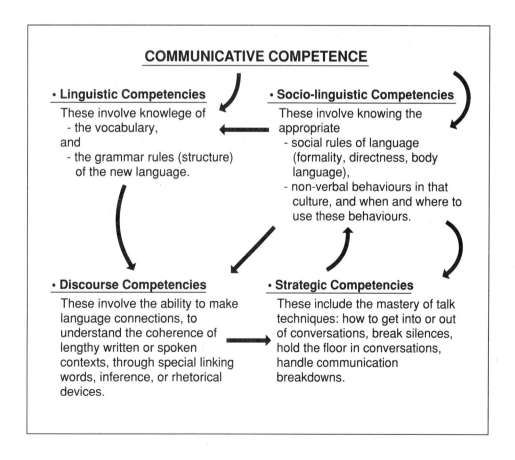

COMMUNICATIVE COMPETENCE

• **Linguistic Competencies**

These involve knowlege of
- the vocabulary,
and
- the grammar rules (structure) of the new language.

• **Socio-linguistic Competencies**

These involve knowing the appropriate
- social rules of language (formality, directness, body language),
- non-verbal behaviours in that culture, and when and where to use these behaviours.

• **Discourse Competencies**

These involve the ability to make language connections, to understand the coherence of lengthy written or spoken contexts, through special linking words, inference, or rhetorical devices.

• **Strategic Competencies**

These include the mastery of talk techniques: how to get into or out of conversations, break silences, hold the floor in conversations, handle communication breakdowns.

The term *Communicative Competence* describes a broad concept of language proficiency. It includes not only linguistic knowledge of grammar, vocabulary and sentence structures but also knowledge of body language and appropriate socio-cultural conventions. It means the ability to speak, to write, to act and to respond in a variety of appropriate ways to different people, in different situations.

QUESTION
Is it any wonder, then, that according to research, it could take five to nine years to become *proficient* in a second language?

Current Programs

The works of Ausubel, Piaget, and Carl Rogers have had a tremendous impact on first-language education as well as on approaches to second-language teaching. I have, however, chosen the work of the influential Soviet psychologist and scholar Lev Vygotsky to conclude this chapter. I did so for several reasons.

First, although Vygotsky lived and worked around the same time as Piaget, his theories on human cognitive development are fairly recent to North American educators. Second, the importance and appeal of Vygotsky's ideas have been gaining steady and serious support in both philosophical and educational institutions in recent years. Third, there is a surge of interest in Vygotsky's work because of North American research findings that support Vygotsky's ideas. Finally, Vygotsky extends our knowledge of human cognition far beyond that of the behaviourists or Piaget's interpretation of biologically based, maturational cognitive processes.

Vygotsky's theories on cognitive development are particularly relevant to second-language teaching because he proposes an explicit and fundamental relationship between social interactions and language and the development of children's potential for thought and higher level thinking processes, i.e., learning and intelligence.

In simplified terms, Vygotsky and his supporters believe that humans are predisposed to socialization. They argue that language and thought and, therefore, further learning, result from the dynamics of the social environment and from the quality of adult/peer verbal interactions and interventions.

The implications of Vygotsky's work, as well as that of Ausubel, Piaget and Rogers, can be found in current approaches within elementary education. The field of second-language teaching has also developed in response to these theories. Active Learning, Integrated Language Learning and Cooperative Learning—all of which have their roots in the humanistic and cognitive domains, are as integral to ESL teaching as they are to regular teaching pedagogy.

Student-centred learning in a risk-free, nurturing environment is good education for all students, not simply for ESL students.

Language proficiency is enhanced for second-language learners in a classroom where ESL students are encouraged to *interact* with native English speakers *during activities where subject matter is being learned*. It is through these daily interactions with peers and during real learning contexts that true communicative competence is supported and developed.

The following chapters further explain the implications that Vygotsky's research and that of his supporters has had for current classroom programming—the practical side of theory. You will perceive the common thread of cognitive, humanistic and social-interaction theories through the incorporation of learning through talk, Active Learning programs, Integrated Language Learning and an emphasis on Cooperative Learning. You will understand how this new "student-centred" philosophy has inexorably changed traditional classroom dynamics.

Finally, subsequent chapters provide you with practical ideas that I hope will be of help to you in providing equal access to a good classroom program for all of your students.

4 Talking and Learning

TALK IS THE MEDIUM
THROUGH WHICH WE
DISCOVER THE CHILD WITHIN.

Figure 4.1

Listening to and recording observations of student talk will tell us, as teachers, a lot more about our students than any test ever will.

Do you remember an instance when talking through something helped you to learn?

- Was it when you had decisions to make—in a relationship, about travel?
- Was it when you couldn't understand the written directions included with all the pieces and wires of your new VCR?
- Was it while coming to grips with the ending of a certain movie, when you wanted to talk about it, to make sense of it?
- Was it when you had to resolve or mediate a conflict?

Talking through ideas helps us clarify and refine our thoughts. Students, at every grade level, will develop a sense of themselves as valued, contributing, important human beings when they are encouraged to share their ideas. For ESL students, this inclusion within the group, their peers and the lesson is particularly important. It is tangible proof that the child is accepted as an individual despite his/her differences.

This inclusion will also encourage ESL students to get involved so that they can acquire and practise their English-language skills in a variety of contexts. This chapter will therefore suggest ways in which we as teachers can begin to nurture student learning through the medium of talk.

A student's language proficiency will affect academic success.

If the above statement is true, then we, as teachers, may be placing our students in jeopardy. Results from a lengthy study of first-language acquisition (Wells 1981) showed that schools were not challenging students with either the same amount of language or the same types of language the children were using in their own homes. In his study, Wells recorded years of data that showed that teachers dominated most conversations and discussions. Teachers were also prone to ask students questions that required rather limited thinking for their answers, i.e., yes-no or simple factual answers. As you saw in Chapter 3, however, ESL students need to use language in order to become truly proficient in English. Moreover, as you also saw in Chapter 3, Vygotsky explicitly ties language to thinking and learning.

Vygotsky's theories of cognitive development stress the importance of
- **social interactions,**
- **verbal guidance,**

and
- **modelling different language functions**

in the development of children's cognitive and intellectual potentials.

Putting Talk on the Curriculum Agenda

In many schools across the country, interventions and practices are being organized to improve student performance in language and literacy.

Example 1

The Flemington Language Project Rationale (Logan and Paige 1987) was developed in response to a study and analysis of Flemington Public School's student achievement results and of the needs of the school's inner-city community in North York. The study, like Vygotsky's research, showed that the most critical ingredient affecting academic achievement was language functioning.

An action-study group in the school identified three areas teachers would work on to support the development of oral language in students:

- the development of the narrative form,
- the influence of teacher and peer interactions,

and

- parent communication and collaboration with the school.

Example 2

There are many ESL students in Firgrove Public School, North York, Ontario, as well. The enrichment of the primary students' oral language in this school was guided and supported by the Vice-Principal, John McCullough. Along with board support staff, McCullough identified mediating strategies that would help move students along a continuum from "social" oral speech to more literate types of language. The key to the program was narratives. Folk tales were chosen as a special focus because they have a repetitive, rhythmic style, making stories easy to remember, and yet they follow a literate type of syntax. Key components of the Firgrove program are shown in Figure 4.2.

Play as Talk, Play as Learning

Not only is play essential to a child's developmental, social and intellectual development, but play offers the perfect situation in which to learn and practise English. If you were to listen to and to record what children were really doing during their play, your list would probably include such language functions as planning, explaining, reporting, directing, justifying, imagining, questioning, reasoning, reflecting, building relationships, dramatizing, storytelling, problem solving, interviewing, arguing, making decisions, persuading, entertaining,

Figure 4.2

The Firgrove Public School teaching staff derived some of the concepts they decided to teach to from the Bracken test. The Bracken test, which was administered as a pre-test, indicated that many children, especially those from low socio-economic backgrounds and/or ESL, did not understand many basic concepts such as spatial terms, opposites, directions and sequencing terms.

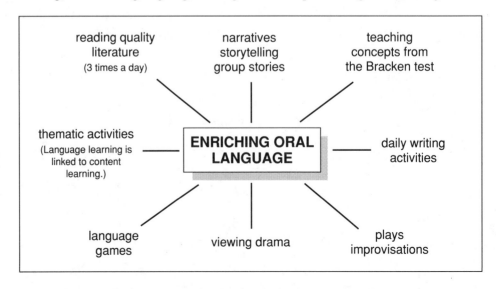

requesting, and expressing emotions (adapted from Lily Wong-Fillmore, quoted in McLaughlin 1985). While at play, ESL students are also learning body language and other important non-verbal communications that we use in our culture (Kramsch 1987).

ESL students need **to learn** and **to use** language within a wide range of contexts. Figure 4.3 suggests some play centres and materials that encourage this variety and range of language.

Figure 4.3

Setting the stage for play: some materials to encourage Play Talk

MATERIALS FOR PLAY TALK

PUPPETS
finger, rod, hand, sock, marionette

HOUSE CENTRE
telephone, dishes, furniture, empty food boxes and tins from a variety of cultures, rice bowls, steamers, cooking utensils, Plasticene for food

DRESS-UP BOX
jewellery, clothing, scarves, saris, masks, helper hats--fire fighter, police, nurse, construction hats, etc.

TOY MONEY
cash registers, coins and money from various countries

TAPE-RECORDER & LISTENING CENTRE
blank tapes, books on tape, instruments

MUSIC
instruments, tapes of songs in different languages

FELT BOARD
props and cutouts, Magnetic Way

GAMES CORNER
partner/group games

COMPUTER AND PRINTER

SAND & WATER TABLES
funnels, hoses, sieves, scoops, shells, rocks, plastic characters and animals

CONSTRUCTION DEPOT
boxes, strings, magazines, clay, tubes, glitter, paper, wallpaper, cans

SCIENTIFIC TABLE
microscope, magnets, models, bug jars, holograms, scales, magnifying glass, cocoons, seeds

WRITING CENTRE
fancy pens, markers, pencils, envelopes, stapler, different colours, sizes and shapes of paper, chalk, stencils

LARGE BLOCKS CONSTRUCTION
blankets, large scarves to create enclosed spaces, blocks of differents sizes and shapes, props

TOYS
garage, city floor map, castle, animals and people, farm or house sets, Lego, dolls of different ethnicity

Providing Models of "Good" English

Some teachers fear that in a class with many second-language learners, students will pick up one another's mistakes in grammar or pronunciation. Many of these teachers are also concerned that they may not have enough native English-speaking students in their classes to provide the necessary fluent language models for the ESL learners. Current research, however, indicates that we shouldn't be concerned about our students learning other students' errors as a result of talk interactions. The chance of this appears to be minimal. (Kramsch 1987 reporting on Porter 1986)

Some Teaching Strategies To Provide English Models

- Partner an activity with a class that has a lot of native English speakers, e.g, trips, surveys and graphs, reading, pen pals, computer networking.
- Invite lots of interaction with guests, e.g, questions to the principal, nurse visits and health programs, visits by artists, storytellers, seniors, board specialists, agencies or business, e.g., Pollution Probe, Environment Canada, etc.
- Plan trips to places or organizations that provide special programs or speakers, such as museums, fairs, galleries. These organizations so often have better resources than you can provide. Also, most places and people will adjust their presentation and timing for ESL groups. Ask ahead for interval time to allow other students to translate important concepts for their ESL classmates.
- Community helpers and hospital visits help new students with cultural adjustment as well as language.
- Make greater use of educational TV programs and videos, movies, books with tapes, etc.
- Read aloud daily from a variety of genres and sources.
- Include many teacher-led, large group lessons. You as teacher can provide the guidance, support and modelling needed for new language structures or vocabulary.

Figure 4.4

Special programs or guests can provide new resources, materials and English-language models for students. Most guides will adjust their presentation and timing for ESL groups.

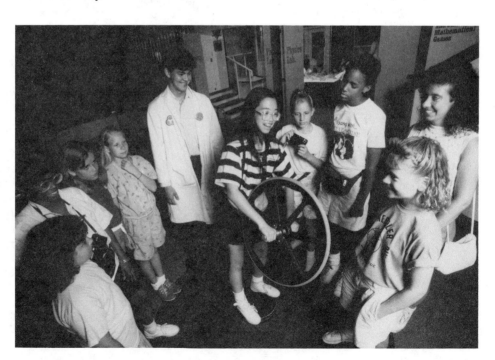

Different Types of Discourse

Just as there are different reasons and styles for writing, there are also different types of speech discourse and different qualities of talk produced during an activity. Consider, for example, the amount and quality of talk (thought involved) in the following examples:

- a student working individually on an assigned worksheet/booklet;
- two students partnered to complete that same worksheet;
- a factual response to a teacher's questioning of content learned;
- a student explanation of what and how he/she learned that content;
- a student-prepared presentation or drama skit about that same content;
- during a student survey;
- in a math problem-solving activity;
- student contributions during large group versus small group activities.

The language that students practise may be limited by the parameters we place on an activity—or by the nature of the activity itself. In many activities, there is a limited range and type of vocabulary that can be expected. In a creative activity, however (e.g., students make up a skit or problem solve), there is unlimited opportunity for language to flow where student interests, experiences and knowledge take it.

When planning a student task, consider ways you can elicit the most on-task, verbal language from that activity.

ESL students need to learn their grade level's subject matter at the same time as they are acquiring proficiency in the English language. In many cases, ESL students will learn new language terms that pertain to special concepts or subjects at the same time as their peers are learning them, e.g., terms for concepts such as evaporation, life cycles, fractions, etc.

Figure 4.5

This figure shows a variety of opportunities for talk in the curriculum.

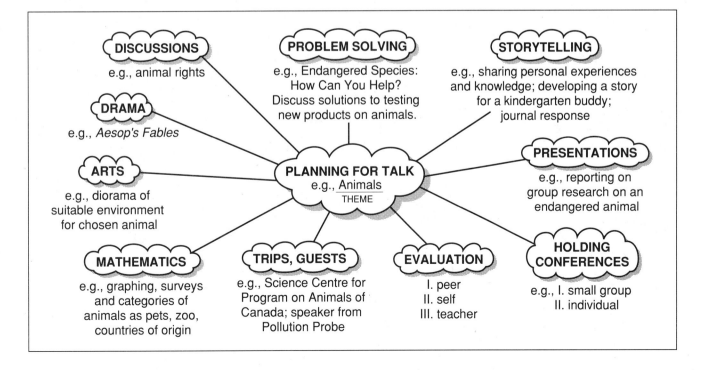

**At certain times, and especially in the junior grades, you will want
your students to *talk on task*. To ensure that the students do so, let the
students know that they must have a specified "product" to share
within a set time.**

In a classroom where talk and language learning are not encouraged, ESL
students will continue to be at a distinct disadvantage, because in our school
system, evaluation of success or progress in a subject is often measured by the
ability to communicate that knowledge. ESL students who are allowed few
opportunities to share, discuss and practise learning through English, will hardly
be able to communicate their knowledge as successfully.

The following chapters will highlight current educational approaches that do
help ESL students acquire language, learn subject content and meet success—
simultaneously. Talk linked to reading, writing and learning in a natural and
supportive fashion is the medium for learning, implicit in each approach.

Active Learning

A ctive Learning means student interaction—with content, with materials and with peers—in a multi-disciplinary, multi-sensory and multi-graded approach. It is a mainstay for student success and a proven strategy for coping with the diversity of student academic levels that challenge many classroom teachers today.

Activities with peers and concrete materials provide the means for ESL students to learn concepts and language at the same time.

In an Active Learning classroom, students are provided with the time, materials and an organized system (classroom routines and expectations) for interaction with their learning. The activities that support students' learning of skills, concepts and language may be in the form of a whole-class grouping, for example, working together with counters in a place value lesson. Or these activities may occur in small groups throughout the classroom and halls. If an activity is set up for any length of time to support a theme or subject, then its location is likely to be known as a "centre"; thus, the terms "activity centre" and/or "learning centre" are often associated with Active Learning methods.

It is important for us as teachers to realize the many and varied ways in which Active Learning programs support second-language learners (as well, of course, as supporting English-speaking students). Figures 5.1 to 5.4 show a number of ways in which an Active Learning program benefits ESL students.

Active Learning, as an approach to overall curriculum presentation,

- advocates a child-centred, experiential mode of *both teaching and learning*; teachers do not abrogate direct teaching situations;
- emphasizes the *process* of learning more than the *product*; teachers guide students to express *how* they learned (metacognitive thinking) as well as to express *what* they learned;
- is interactive by nature, with peers, with the subject matter and with materials; this process is usually termed "hands-on" experience;

How Active Learning Specifically Benefits ESL Children

Figure 5.1

 Active Learning takes into account **different rates of learning.** *Activities tend to include open-ended tasks for multi-level learning opportunities. All students, including ESL, special education and exceptional students, can access learning at their own levels.*

Figure 5.2

Active Learning allows for **different learning styles.** *Various types of activities are designed to allow for experiential, multi-sensory modes of receiving and producing communications. This variety also provides "hooks," or meaningful contexts, to help students retain new language.*

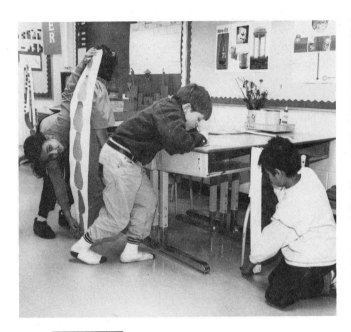

Figure 5.3

Active Learning relies on collaboration among students. *Activities encourage interaction about a task which, in turn, enhances students' language and thinking skills. This group inclusion will also help ESL students feel accepted and integrated. Students' differences and their strengths will be recognized and valued.*

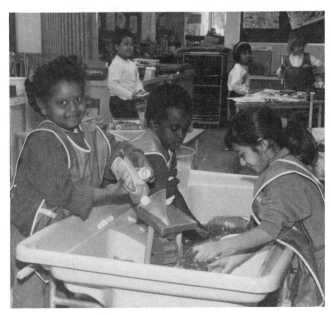

Figure 5.4

Active Learning allows for essential "output" *opportunities. At centres, the ESL students practise* using the language *they need in different contexts.*

- integrates the four language skills of listening, speaking, reading and writing with a topic, and may encompass other subject areas; learning is, therefore, integrated or holistic;
- connects learning and language to real situations so ESL students will find English more meaningful, versus a reliance on textbooks or worksheets;
- promotes responsibility and ownership of their learning in the students by providing opportunities for them to make choices in what and how they will learn;
- incorporates thematic units; the "Language Experience Approach" to reading instruction (see Chapter 9, "What To Do When They Arrive Brand New"); centres that allow for different learning strengths; manipulatives; large blocks of time; and a variety of grouping techniques—all of which benefit ESL students;
- implies that teachers will develop skills in record-keeping and tracking of student skills development and in the observation of students for planning and evaluation purposes.

In Active Learning programs, we, as teachers, make decisions about which activities and centres to set up based on the requirements of our curriculum and on the needs and interests of our particular students. Observing our students is an important feature of Active Learning so that we can create new and meaningful tasks and lessons as the needs arise. For example, we can plan activity centres to help students with specific literacy skills in reading and writing or for speaking (collaborative talk) to practise using the thematic vocabulary; we can set up centres to nurture broader creativity through students' choices in following their interests or strengths, such as art, drama, music, etc.

It is also essential to have a range of materials accessible that will assist ESL students to move along a continuum in their understanding of new ideas and vocabulary, i.e., going from the real object, to the pictorial, to the symbolic or abstract representation, as in the written word.

As we saw in Chapter 3, second-language learners must have multiple opportunities to practise *using* new language structures and terms that are taught in the different subject areas.

As teachers, therefore, we should plan activities that create opportunities for talking: collaborative talk in discussions, problem solving, sharing news or stories, conferencing, analyzing, evaluating, presenting—all of which provide the ESL student with essential practice using the new vocabulary and concepts of your topic in meaningful ways. In addition, activities of this sort make effective use of other English sources available to ESL students—fellow peers who will model appropriate language use.

Children use language to learn, but they are also learning about language at the same time.

Figure 5.5

The Teacher's Role in Active Learning

Issues in Active Learning

"But child-centred classrooms seem so noisy!"
   There are few other life situations that are as artificial as a traditional classroom. Normally, people talk together, cooperate and collaborate, work or play on teams and get help from multiple sources. Human beings are dependent on interaction and need it to grow mentally, socially and emotionally.

—Collinson (1991)

   Active Learning in classrooms is crucial to successful second-language teaching and learning. There are several issues and certain common problems that may, however, interfere with actual benefits that second-language learners can derive from this type of program, and these will be discussed here.

Critics of Active Learning argue that there is not enough substance to the program, that there is nothing going on but "play," even in the junior grades, and that children aren't being "moved along" in their skills development. In essence, the argument against Active Learning is twofold: that "play" is not learning, and that teachers aren't teaching.

But, in good Active Learning programs, teachers structure their activities with careful attention to curriculum demands *and* student abilities.

Active Learning involves much more than just setting up certain permanent centres. e.g., arts and crafts, drama, writing and reading centres. In the best Active Learning programs, centres are incorporated with classroom curriculum; they are not simply a choice of activity once a student's "regular" work is completed. For each new curricular topic, we, as teachers, should consider how we can restructure existing centres, or what new centres we might add, to help students conceptualize, practise, rehearse and re-use or recycle the concepts and language for that new concept or that theme. For example, we may adapt one or more permanent centres to suit the new theme—we may add a stack of new easy readers and pictorial books on the topic to the reading centre for second-language learners, use the arts centre for a shoebox diorama that will demonstrate a student's knowledge of new language and concepts taught, or revamp the house centre into a store to consolidate the concepts and language from the money theme in mathematics.

Accountability is an integral feature of Active Learning programs—accountability for students, while they work through a series of centres, and accountability for teachers, to fulfil that grade level's curricular requirements. As educators and for parents, *we must ensure that children do experience learning while at their "play" and that students do indeed progress along a continuum of skills*. Therefore, a system that tracks student outcomes through centres alone is not adequate. Tracking procedures should also include observations of students' social and cognitive levels throughout each term, so that change or progress can be discerned. Our observations of second-language learners during groupwork is also an excellent way to evaluate their progress in language and socialization.

Good tracking is, therefore, descriptive of what a student can do, and also prescriptive, in that the tracking will show us what skills, language or behaviours that particular student is ready to learn next.

Activities are planned that reflect both the skill needs of students and the content and concepts to be taught for that grade.

It is also important for us to include direct teaching experiences where we can introduce new concepts, model appropriate language and terms, guide student thinking, evaluate student knowledge or help students reflect on their prior learning. This can be done in a variety of groupings—in whole class and in small group settings. Ideally, while students are actively and meaningfully engaged in their centre work, we will be able to lead smaller groups in skills development, do comprehension checks, record observations of students, or assist students with developing their own personal work sample portfolios. Small group situations will also allow us to attend to our weaker second-language learners' special needs for vocabulary or content review.

There will no doubt be certain students who have difficulty coping with the talk, movement, and individual and social demands of Active Learning classrooms. Although most students operate very well in such an environment, we must also recognize that some students will require a teacher to limit their choices and freedoms with a more structured and modified program, perhaps even within their own space. This modification of the program is perfectly legitimate and remains child-centred as it is suited to the needs of those particular children.

One School's Assessment of Active Learning

In one particular school with 70% second-language learners, the administration and staff had been focusing on the needs of ESL students for several years. The previous year, Active Learning had been singled out as a key area to address the needs of integrated ESL students. It became obvious throughout the year, however, that Active Learning was not being implemented in all classrooms and then only in certain subject areas. This awareness became the impetus for the teachers' and administration's next professional activity session in which staff were instructed to discuss and clarify, in small groups, what Active Learning meant to them. When group ideas were charted and posted in the follow-up sharing session, certain commonalities and recurring teacher concerns were obvious and, therefore, noted.

In every grade level, teachers recognized the need to establish clear routines early in the year, and to direct their students' attention to expectations for that class regarding the social skills necessary in Active Learning programs, such as cooperation, sharing, problem solving and decision making.

In every group, teachers also expressed a concern over the ongoing need for funding to purchase or replace materials and for adequate space, the lack of which consistently handicapped their implementation of Active Learning. Additionally, all the teachers in this busy school wanted to see an improvement in the support systems for teachers and in the ways of presenting professional development.

It was very clear that these teachers believed in the value of coming together to dialogue and work in teams, and in sharing the many strengths of existing staff members. But these people also stated that they needed to find more creative ways to meet together, instead of using so many of their lunch hours. Several teachers commented that the many ongoing initiatives at noon hour sapped their time and emotional reserves, so that upon returning to their classrooms and students after lunch, they were feeling drained and stressed, instead of alert and prepared. It is easy to extrapolate from this that some teachers feeling this pressure could forget to exude a friendly, welcoming front should a new, non-English speaking child be escorted to their classroom that afternoon.

The teachers expressed a hope that the administration would support them in their desire to direct their own professional activities, as well as in the creative use of time for teachers to help one another through dialogue and planning teams. During this session, the school administration reaffirmed its belief in the teachers' commitment to improving not only the quality of student learning but the quality of their own professional lives. The aim of this meeting had been to refocus teachers' attention on educating through Active Learning, but the outcome was a vociferous plea for the empowerment of individual teachers and teams of teachers in their grass roots efforts to program effectively for students.

Four Schemata To Assist in Planning and Developing Active Learning Programs

Active Learning is the best way of presenting the regular curriculum.

1. Active Learning Planning Sheet

Experiences are the foundations for building language and further learning (Wells 1974).

Activity centres can either provide an initial experience or capitalize on a previous experience. By going back to a favourite centre and by working in thematic-related centres, students will build on their knowledge in a cyclical or spiral approach to learning, i.e., students will expand and consolidate their current knowledge each time they meet the topic and vocabulary in the various centre tasks. Figure 5.6 (page 47) provides a sample planning sheet for planning theme-based centres in multi-sensory and multi-disciplinary modes. The sheet is reproduced as Blackline Master #5.

2. Brainstorming Program Ideas

Brainstorming a flow chart or web is a popular method for developing program activities. Ideas can be organized under subject areas. Or you can concentrate on providing varied experiences to consolidate one particular topic. Examples of each type of web are shown in Figures 5.7 and 5.8 (pages 48 and 49 respectively).

3. Planning for Learning Styles

An easy definition of Learning Styles is *the preferred ways in which an individual receives and processes information.* Planning for different learning styles allows students to develop potentials in different areas, and to appreciate different strengths in other people.

A program attentive to learning styles is best for ESL students because it implies:

- different types of groupings, which offer support in language acquisition from different peers and in a variety of language contexts;
- extensive use of visuals and various graphic techniques to assist comprehension, e.g., charts, graphs, drawings, models, kits;
- multi-sensory and experiential activities that provide a "scaffold" to assist the learning of concepts as well as language.

Howard Gardner, Harvard Professor of Education and Developmental Psychologist, wrote an influential book, *The Theory of Multiple Intelligences,* in which he describes seven areas of intelligence:

- **Linguistic**—people who read and write well. They are attuned to language, e.g., authors, poets;
- **Logical-Mathematical**—people with strengths as logical and abstract thinkers, who recognize patterns easily, e.g., scientists, logicians;
- **Musical**—people who love and show sensitivity to pitch, melody, rhythm and tone, e.g., musicians, conductors;
- **Bodily-Kinesthetic**—people with athletic abilities, or who can use their body skillfully, e.g., dancers, actors, artisans, athletes;

THEME: FAIRY TALES AND FOLK TALES

Jot down related activities in each column. Then select and sequence the ideas in weekly plans. Highlight ideas you will need advice/help with. Cross off each area as you transfer the centres to a weekly planning sheet.

MAIN CONCEPTS	SENSORY EXPERIENCES	PERFORMING ARTS	ARTS & CRAFTS	GUESTS &/ or TRIPS
• *literacy skills development* • *values education related to moral issues in Fairy Tales* • *exposing students to the genre and language of Fairy Tales* • *all cultures have storytelling*	e.g. sight, hearing, taste, touch, smell • *cooking bean soup* • *symphonies for Peter and The Wolf and the Nutcracker Suite* • *songs*	e.g., music, creative movement, dance, demonstrations, gymnastics • *Nutcracker Ballet* • *Beauty and the Beast* • *Young People's Theatre*	e.g., mask-making, clay, design, constructions • *character puppets* • *dioramas of story setting* • *clay modelling* • *costumes*	• *Casa Loma* • *Hobberlin Centre* • *Puppet Museum* • *storyteller*
AUDIO-VISUAL	**SHARING TIMES**	**DRAMA**	**PROBLEM SOLVING**	**COMPUTER PROGRAM**
e.g., kits, movies, videos, TV • *make own story tapes* • *Cinderella video* • *Beauty & the Beast* • *Aladdin*	e.g., show & tell, collections, discussions, student presentations • *process work accomplished* • *celebration of students who learn to read* • *fairy tales comparisons*	e.g., skits, readers, theatre, tableaux, mime • *act out stories and their own plays* • *drama centre*	e.g., issues, action • *values issues* • *are all stepmothers bad* • *are all wolves bad* • *environmental concerns* • *brutality, and good vs evil*	• *word-processing programs* • *story-building program*
STORIES/ ARTICLES	**WRITING IDEAS**	**RELATED MATH SKILLS**	**ENVIRONMENTAL STUDIES**	**SCIENCE**
• *books* • *units of study* • *professional guides* • *progression of materials from pictures and non-writing only to complete story*	• *rewrite endings* • *write/pattern* • *picture only* • *word sentence* • *paint picture & tell story about it* • *retelling* • *response journal*	• *measurement, sizing, graphing & collage of shoes/beans* • *graph fairy tales* • *fairy tale math* • *recipes—fractions*	e.g., concepts, issues, materials • *research castles* • *on authors* • *Hans Christian Anderson* • *map storyline and setting* • *landscapes*	e.g., kits, equipment, concepts • *planting beans re Jack & the Beanstalk* • *mystery powders re magic potion*
PHONETIC & SPELLING SKILLS	**NEW VOCABULARY OR TERMS**	**HOME ACTIVITIES**	**NOTES**	
e.g., cross-reference with computer programs • *thematic spelling C sound as in Cinderella*	• *fairy tale words* • *opposites, e.g., good-evil, right-wrong*	• *reading* • *sharing cultural tales* • *questioning*	*Fact, Fantasy, and Folklore: Expanding Language Arts and Critical Thinking Skills by Lipson, Morrison and Swanson* ← *Get Copy* *Bloom's Taxonomy*	

Figure 5.6

Sample Active Learning Planning Sheet for Theme-based Activity Centres: Fairy Tales and Folk Tales. Derived from **English as a Second Language K-12. Resource Book, Vol. 1. Integrating Language and Content Instruction**. *British Columbia, Ministry of Education, 1987.*

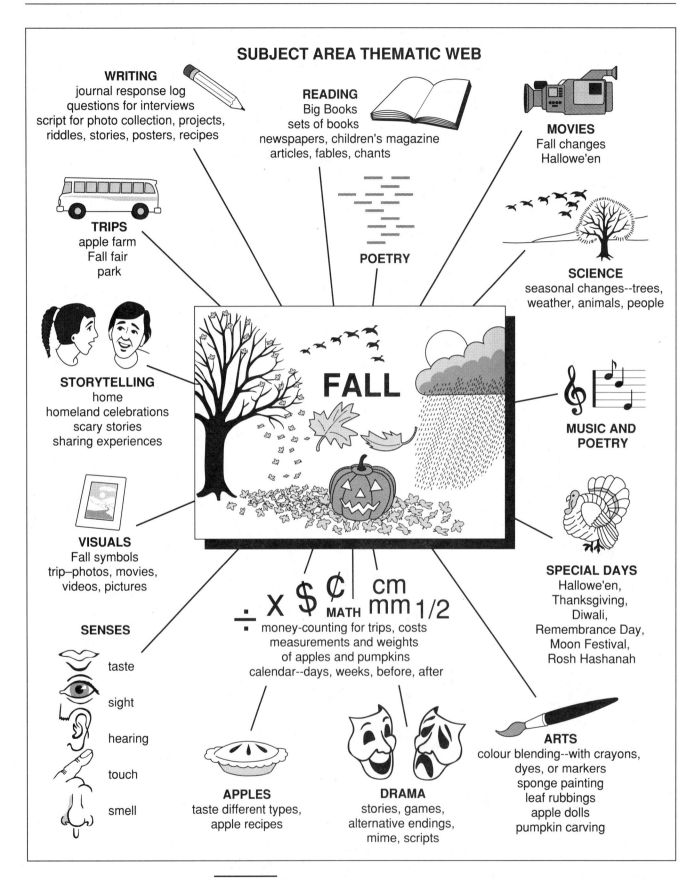

SUBJECT AREA THEMATIC WEB

WRITING
journal response log
questions for interviews
script for photo collection, projects,
riddles, stories, posters, recipes

READING
Big Books
sets of books
newspapers, children's magazine
articles, fables, chants

MOVIES
Fall changes
Hallowe'en

TRIPS
apple farm
Fall fair
park

POETRY

SCIENCE
seasonal changes--trees,
weather, animals, people

STORYTELLING
home
homeland celebrations
scary stories
sharing experiences

FALL

MUSIC AND POETRY

VISUALS
Fall symbols
trip–photos, movies,
videos, pictures

SPECIAL DAYS
Hallowe'en,
Thanksgiving,
Diwali,
Remembrance Day,
Moon Festival,
Rosh Hashanah

SENSES
taste
sight
hearing
touch
smell

MATH
money-counting for trips, costs
measurements and weights
of apples and pumpkins
calendar--days, weeks, before, after

APPLES
taste different types,
apple recipes

DRAMA
stories, games,
alternative endings,
mime, scripts

ARTS
colour blending--with crayons,
dyes, or markers
sponge painting
leaf rubbings
apple dolls
pumpkin carving

Figure 5.7

Sample Subject Area Thematic Web: Fall

Figure 5.8

Sample Topic Thematic Web: Money

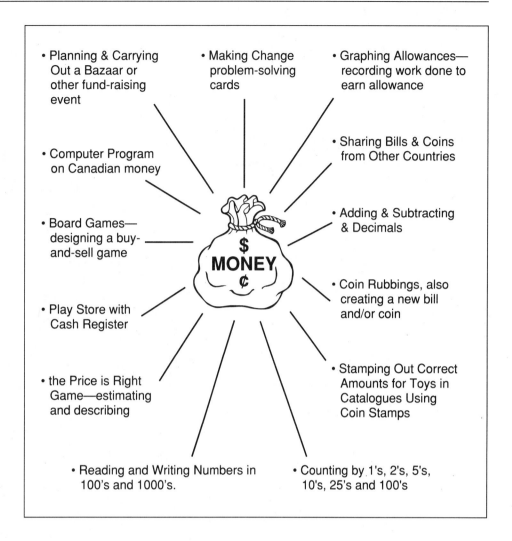

- Planning & Carrying Out a Bazaar or other fund-raising event
- Making Change problem-solving cards
- Graphing Allowances— recording work done to earn allowance
- Computer Program on Canadian money
- Sharing Bills & Coins from Other Countries
- Board Games— designing a buy-and-sell game
- Adding & Subtracting & Decimals
- Play Store with Cash Register
- Coin Rubbings, also creating a new bill and/or coin
- the Price is Right Game—estimating and describing
- Stamping Out Correct Amounts for Toys in Catalogues Using Coin Stamps
- Reading and Writing Numbers in 100's and 1000's.
- Counting by 1's, 2's, 5's, 10's, 25's and 100's

- **Spatial**—people who perceive the world accurately and can re-create or transform aspects of that world, e.g., architects, artists, scientists;
- **Interpersonal**—people with leadership qualities, empathy and the ability to understand people and relationships; they demonstrate high social skill, e.g., diplomats, business people, counsellors, editors;
- **Intrapersonal**—people with strong introspective personalities. They are "in tune" with their inner feelings and need "space" to develop in their own ways, e.g., writers, business people.

Gardner, who has investigated intelligence and human potentials for many years and across many cultures, holds expansive views on both. Why, he argues, should one area be called a talent and another, an intelligence? Schools, he adds, are biased in favour of two areas of intelligence: linguistic and logical-mathematical. Gardner argues that human potentials will only be realized if we provide opportunities for students to develop and share their other areas of intelligence as well. *Like Vygotsky, Gardner sees education as a social medium, in that the whole group benefits from sharing the special abilities of the individuals.*

Figure 5.9 suggests some ways we can plan to accommodate different learning styles and to nurture the various types of intelligence.

THEORY OF MULTIPLE INTELLIGENCES

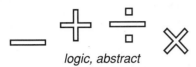

logic, abstract

LOCIGAL--MATHEMATICAL

Plan for--classifying, ordering (sequence),
reasoning activities, science kits, patterns,
computer games, strategy games

words, books, poetry, stories

LINGUISTIC

Plan for--reading, writing, word games, spelling,
storytelling, discussions, verbal tasks

*visualization, imagery,
charts, maps*

SPATIAL

Plan for--constructing, drawing,
graphing, map-making,
blocks, Lego, crafts, models,
use of graphic organizers (visual maps)
for reading and assignments

*self-awareness & knowledge,
reflective, self-motivated*

INTRAPERSONAL

Plan for--individualized learning opportunities,
e.g., reading, journals, solo research,
diaries, choice, quiet times

social, interaction, group dynamics

INTERPERSONAL

Plan for--group and partner tasks, peer/cross-grade tutoring,
games, leadership skills, Cooperative Learning opportunities

touching, sensing, movement, experimenting

BODILY-KINESTHETIC

Plan for--hands-on tasks, manipulatives,
crafts, blocks, drama, dance and movement
activities, sports, physical education areas,
typewriter/computer for writing

instruments, appreciation, rhythm, sounds

MUSICAL

Plan for--choral work (reading), singing,
rhythm activities, soundscapes to poetry and stories,
lummi sticks, listening centre materials, choir, chants

Figure 5.9

*Planning To Accommodate Different Learning Styles and To Nurture Multiple
Intelligences (derived from Howard Gardner, **The Theory of Multiple Intelligences**)*

4. Themeboxes—Preparation of Materials

The following idea relieves individual teachers of the onerous task of program planning and materials preparation for Active Learning in every subject area, and for new grade levels.

It does, however, require a collaborative effort by interested staff to meet, to decide on a unit and to brainstorm appropriate thematic activities. Each teacher then prepares one of the activities. All of the activities are housed in a central box that teachers share by signing out several idea bags at a time for their own classroom use.

Each activity is stored in a large plastic baggie. Enough copies are made of any one activity for all the students at the centre concerned. Teachers who borrow the Themebox do not have to make extra copies because everything is included and ready to use.

In one such cooperative effort at Gateway Public School in North York, Ontario, teachers planned and prepared a variety of centres that would develop student awareness of the symbols, customs and language of Hallowe'en as well as furthering student literacy skills. Activities were developed, suited for Grades 1 through 5.

The activities included

- a tape and booklet of Hallowe'en songs and chants;
- a bag with a simple feltboard story and felt cutouts for stories;
- eight large, colourful, Hallowe'en poster pictures, cut up and placed in separate baggies for a puzzle centre;
- five sets of Hallowe'en riddles that student partners manipulate to match the answers to the riddle cards;
- Hallowe'en stamp sets for making cards and notes;
- four spooky stories on tapes;
- a good selection of beautiful visual Hallowe'en storybooks;
- research questions focused on bats, ghosts and witches;
- a reproducible ghost fold-up shape with lines inside for stories;
- bags of cut-up cardboard letters for Hallowe'en spelling;
- Hallowe'en word cards with matching pictures for grouping into the numbers of syllables;
- bags of pumpkin seeds for a review of multiplication (three times table);
- measurement cards for pumpkins;
- various arts and crafts ideas on laminated activity cards;
- four sets of cookie cutters;
- two sets of Hallowe'en lacing picture cards for primary students;
- several matching activity sets of Hallowe'en pictures and words;
- a reference binder of additional Hallowe'en language arts ideas.

When teachers come across a new idea, they add it to the box.

The best activities for learning are those that involve students physically and collaboratively, in other words, activities that involve the manipulation of materials, verbalization of ideas and work with peers.

Integrated Language Learning

Integrated Language Learning refers to *both language acquisition and learning in general*. It calls for a student-centred curriculum taught through interrelating the skills of listening, speaking, reading and writing with a topic. The Integrated Language Learning approach challenges traditional practices of teaching literacy, i.e., teaching skills in reading and writing, as separate and often non-verbal entities. In fact, Integrated Language Learning extends far beyond "reading" or "writing." It is based on a philosophical belief of how children learn best and how good teaching should, therefore, proceed. Integrated Language Learning advocates a new orientation to the presentation and practice of content and skills.

Language, further learning and literacy are viewed as a continuously interacting phenomenon*.

In practice, viewing language, further learning, and literacy in this way means vocabulary, phonetics and grammar skills are not taught in a vacuum, i.e., as an unrelated subject, but rather *according to the readiness level of students and as those skills arise in other learning contexts*. We teachers guide children to create meaningful connections between skills and real examples of their use in a piece of reading or writing: we do not present that skill simply because it is the next topic page of a reader or phonics workbook. Moreover, we integrate language with learning in other subjects by planning for the continuous interaction of all the language skills—listening, speaking, reading and writing: not by isolating these skills by timeslot or subject.

There are many prevalent terms for methods that are based on or are related in ideology to the Integrated Language Learning approach. Some such terms are holistic learning, Whole Language programming, Reading-Writing Classrooms, Literature-Based programs, or Child-Centred Classrooms.

(*A term I borrowed and extended from Gruenewald and Pollak's view of language 1990)

What Does Integrated Language Learning Assume?

1. Intrinsic Motivation

- Children must *connect* to the skills of reading, writing, listening and speaking being taught. For the children to connect to their learning, the learning activity must be meaningful. In other words, reading, for example, is related to some past knowledge and/or present experience; it is not the activity of the day because it happens to be the next story in a reader. This connection is actively developed when we use the Integrated Language Learning approach. Collaborative talk and inclusion, especially important for ESL students, are built in because children are encouraged to share their backgrounds, beliefs and expectations of the topic or story.

- Integrated Language Learning also assumes that the activity is of **interest** to students. Materials chosen for Integrated Language Learning reading programs include stories, articles, songs, raps and poetry that relate to the age, cognition, and culture, in short, to the lives of the students involved. Integrated Language Learning allows for a huge range of source materials and topics to choose from—storybooks, magazines, music, personal, environmental and political issues, holidays, love, friendships, etc.

2. Student Involvement

- There is an assumption that when children connect to an activity they will do so *actively*. Therefore, Integrated Language Learning subsumes Active Learning. Children will chime in to add the predictable next line in a story, they will chant back, vocalize ideas, and experience an activity while talking, writing and reading about it.

Figure 6.1

After going on a trip to a nearby park, the students and teacher wrote a chart story about their experiences. The visuals, spacing and use of colour support the development of the children's literacy skills.

3. A Top-down Approach

- Students start with the *totality of meaning*—the whole story or experience. The joy and connections to a story or activity come first.
- The investigation of the story for word choice, cohesion, phonetic purposes (rhyme, sound-letter correspondence) is introduced and taught as *a natural follow-up* to that particular experience. Phonics is addressed because the particular *skills relate to the chosen reading piece* and second, because *the students indicate their readiness for these skills*. For example, the primary picture book *Fire, Fire* by Gail Gibbons is a great way to investigate rhyming words *but only after* students have enjoyed the humour and rhythm of the story.
- For ESL children, following up a reading experience with further language arts activities not only reinforces the new language and grammar structures, it also ensures greater comprehension. When ESL students practise new vocabulary, sentence patterns or phonetic skills, these language tasks become more meaningful as they are linked to a story, concepts or events. Ausubel's Cognitive Learning Theory and Krashen's Comprehensible Input theory (Chapter 3) stress that good teaching builds on what children already know. **Meaning precedes understanding.** All students need to know what concepts or vocabulary mean before they can develop a further, deeper understanding of them. ESL students need reading, writing and talking activities that support literacy experiences. These connections will help ESL students to incorporate new language into their own English use.

The traditional phonetic approach to reading works with some students whose learning styles are linguistically oriented, who are auditory learners and who have had rich background experiences with the English language. A heavy emphasis on phonetics, however, does not address the needs of the vast majority of second-language learners in the areas of language acquisition or comprehension. Integrated Language Learning methodologies do meet these needs and, at the same time, include phonics as *one* aspect of literacy.

---

4. Integrated Language Skills

In Integrated Language classrooms, the four skill areas of listening, speaking, reading and writing are so intertwined that it's difficult to perceive which task started the other. Writing is reading after all. We read what we write. We write ideas after we talk about them. We extend and reshape our ideas while listening to others.

This *integration or mixing of language skills* enables ESL students to see the connections between words that are spoken and language that is written and read. Reading and writing become more comprehensible when related directly with the talked-about experience. ESL students learn so much about the purposes and varieties of language through guided practice with experience charts, pattern books, poetry and song lyrics.

5. Acceptance of Every Child

Every class has students with different abilities, different levels of skills acquisition, different levels of language fluency and different strengths to offer and learn through.

- In Integrated Language programs, teachers are very accepting of these differences and consider them while **providing for all children, at their level, in the class activities**.

  Every child will benefit by being read to from the selection that he or she is going to study, just as all children will benefit from their peers while sharing experiences and ideas. In such a program, second-language learners of different abilities acquire skills alongside peers with different abilities, as they all become actively involved with many opportunities to hear, practise and record a variety of language (especially the rich language of high quality books).

- Accepting every child's rate and ability to learn also assumes that programs will be planned that offer a variety of choices for students to plug into. Many teachers find that *literature-based programming* is an excellent strategy for implementing Integrated Language Learning because literacy skills can be presented while learning another subject. One junior classroom, for example, comprising over 50% second-language students, used visual Big Books to present the concepts for that grade level's investigations in science.

Results from a variety of studies indicate that literature-based reading programs, versus basal readers, are particularly successful in teaching ESL, disabled and disinterested readers (Tunnell and Jacobs 1989).

One experiment in which a literature-based program was used in the kindergartens involved an elementary school in New York City. The school's student clientele comprised 92% ESL students and 96% of the families lived below the poverty level. School officials were so impressed with the results that they eventually extended the program through all grade levels.

I suggest a few literature-based lessons that can be used to provide for a variety of learning levels and student choices at the end of this chapter.

Open-ended tasks, experiential activities and learning centres allow students to successfully access learning at their own level.

What Happens in Integrated Language Programs?

• Use of Natural Texts

In Integrated Language Learning classrooms, reading materials are very eclectic. There is an effort to present different facets of language use so that students will experience spoken and written texts that reflect the diversity and richness of human language. Thus, language acquisition will be enhanced for ESL students with the range of language presented through "real" storybooks, poetry, articles and language experience charts, versus a reliance on basal reader stories.

• Listening to Stories Read Aloud by the Teacher

This includes more than a daily story read for pleasure. It also means that sometimes the students are read to from the piece they are to work on or study. In this way, students who have difficulty with the reading vocabulary can still

Fig. 6.2

What Goes On in an Integrated Language Learning Classroom

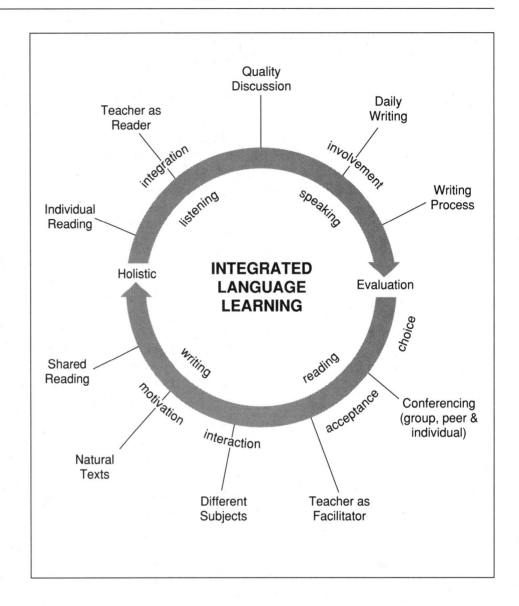

enjoy the selection and learn the ideas and concepts before tackling the piece on their own in further activities. ESL children will also learn much from the intonation, rhythm and inflection that a teacher uses while reading.

• Shared Reading

Shared reading assumes several or all students read in unison, call out or chant sections of the chosen selection. Sharing the experience of reading in small or large groups encourages ESL students to take risks in using language. They won't feel as vulnerable to ridicule.

There are two types of Shared Reading:
1. Group reading—using Big Books, songs, book sets, charts;
2. Partner reading—free choice or teacher-determined texts.

• Individual Reading

Every classroom should include daily time for students to read self-selected material. In fact, time spent on reading is directly related to student success in tests, vocabulary strengths and overall achievement (Tunnell and Jacobs 1989).

• Quality Discussions

We, as teachers, should encourage our students to talk about what and how they are learning. ESL students can learn so much more about language if they become involved in talk with peers that develops and extends an experience or story. In his *Theory of Multiple Intelligences* (Chapter 3), Howard Gardner talks about the importance of assisting students to reflect on their learning, about leading children to be mindful of not only *what* they learned, but *how* they learned it. He challenges us as educators to provoke reflection, judgments and decision making in our students. This process is called *metacognition*.

During class meetings and sharing times, our questions can elicit answers that show reflection, preferences, opinions, explanations, and implications. The learning from an experience or a good book can be enhanced even further by the discussion that surrounds it, that focuses or highlights for second-language learners interesting ideas and uses of language.

• Daily Writing

Integrated Language Learning provides ESL students with a variety of opportunities to write for a variety of purposes: to take notes, plan, invite, show comprehension, explain, reflect, tell a story, or to share ideas for others to see, e.g., for posting or to put in book form. ESL students will learn how writing is used in different contexts. Writing, as integrated with other subject areas, will provide ESL children with the practice necessary to retain new vocabulary and grammar structures.

Meanwhile, a sample of an ESL student's writing will tell us a great deal about that child's level of English skills and general proficiency. It is often in a piece of writing that we will first perceive a child's difficulties with language, difficulties that we had not noted in oral speech. Verb tense errors, run-on sentences, lack of cohesive devices, incorrect pronunciation, etc., are common ESL written errors that *signal special needs*. A work sample portfolio of an ESL student's writing will demonstrate that student's progress as he or she develops language and skills. These samples will also indicate those skills the student is ready to learn next in a group lesson or through conferencing.

• Holistic Evaluation

In holistic evaluation, we rely on a combination of observations and judgments over a period of time and consider *all* areas of a student's growth in learning. Holistic evaluation is especially crucial for ESL students because the end product of a student's work, therefore, comprises only one part of many in forming the overall evaluation. Equally important for evaluative purposes is the learning process that each child goes through in completing that end product: the progression and development of social skills, literacy skills, language acquisition and attitudes.

Holistic evaluation also usually includes several types of student self-evaluation. We, as teachers, often guide verbal evaluations with our classes by setting aside time for students to talk together about what and how they did an assignment: the successes, the strategies used and the problems with a task. Additionally, students might evaluate their work and learning in a response journal, using our questions to guide their thinking. We may also have students use a checklist or comment form to focus the students' attention on their development of academic and/or social skills.

We may encourage our students to create their own portfolios comprising self- and group evaluations, teacher conference notes, along with tracking or checklist sheets, dated work samples, and teacher anecdotes, all of which allow students and parents to see progress.

You may find Blackline Masters #1, 2, and 3, "Classroom Teacher's List of Strategies That Enhance Second-Language Acquisition: Atmosphere (#1), Program (#2), and Interaction (#3)," helpful as you set up your Integrated Language Learning classroom or as you re-evaluate how well your Integrated Language Learning program is working.

Second-Language Learners as Writers

It takes time for second-language learners to develop the confidence to write personally and even more time for ESL learners to develop enough English facility to write creatively. Generally speaking, there is a noticeable breakthrough or leap in the *independent* writing abilities of ESL students one to three years after they first arrive in our schools.

Students with good literacy skills in their first language might start writing short pieces *independently* during the last half of their first year in English schools. This writing, however, should be a reflection of their current studies or of class discussions. It will also be easier for them to write if several models have been provided, e.g., a whole-class experience chart, working with the ideas and vocabulary in centres, during small group and teacher-led writing activities.

The following are some methods you may find helpful in easing new ESL students into your writing program:

- at writing times and at centres, if possible, pair a new student with a buddy who speaks the same first language;
- have the student write ideas on the topics in his/her first language and get the work translated;
- have the student make a list of the important content words for your themes which then can be translated at home and studied;
- treat errors in their writing *only if they affect meaning*—don't draw attention to all the grammatical, spelling and punctuation errors; gradually, students will attend to these aspects through good daily modelling and group/individual feedback in conferencing lessons;
- remember that *meaning precedes learning*. New topics, and certainly new cultural phenomena, should be translated so the ESL student will be able to make sense of ideas before writing. For example, in order for a new ESL student to write a letter to Santa, even in his or her first language, the child should be instructed who this Santa is, what results are hoped for from the written letter, and how this all fits in with North American culture. It is also important to allow the students some choice in their selection of a topic; writing to Santa may still not be meaningful or of interest, even after ESL students have understood the concept;
- teach writing as a process;
- model writing conferences.

Writing as a Process

It is particularly helpful for ESL students if we, as teachers, instruct and model for them how writing is really a series of steps—**a process**. What follows is a suggestion on how to model for ESL students, the sequence, skills and language involved with writing as a process. This method of teaching writing skills is very supportive for second-language students because of each of the intermediary steps which provide suggestions, help and guidance.

First, prepare to model a sample writing exercise. Plan to present the techniques involved with process writing in daily sessions over the span of a week. Look ahead at each step to remind yourself of which terms may be new and/or difficult for second-language learners. When presenting the lessons, rephrase these new terms in order to clarify their meanings; as well, list them on a class reference chart.

IN YOUR MODEL LESSONS:

    1. model pre-writing activities to generate ideas (e.g., brainstorming, webs);
    2. write a story draft on a large chart (on alternate lines);
    3. conference with students for feedback on your work;
    4. show students how you revise and edit the draft copy;
    5. discuss sharing the final copy of your writing in an appropriate form.

WRITING CONFERENCES

Before having your students meet in a writing conference, model appropriate conference etiquette. It is important to help ESL students, in particular, to learn how to frame feedback in a positive way. In a pretend lesson, demonstrate ways

Figure 6.3

Students are sharing their knowledge and language facility, having previously brainstormed words, phrases and facts related to the topic of wolves. The list will serve as a basis for further language development and writing activites. Note the use of visuals alongside the words.

of saying things that might hurt other students' feelings or confidence. Then as an alternative, have the class make several compliments about the work. Next, ask the class to suggest ways to provide constructive criticisms and chart these ideas for future reference.

You might guide your students to start their suggestions with

- I think I would understand your story better if...
- What do you think about trying...
- I like...but....

1. To begin a conference, have students *read their work through once* to their partner, in its entirety. The partner should listen for the meaning of the story, i.e., does the story make sense in English?

   Despite your modelling of conference etiquette, some conferencing partners may exhibit a compulsive tendency to change the wording and mark all the errors in the work of students who are beginning English writers. This approach is not conducive to helping the new student's confidence, motivation or retention of the suggestions. In cases like this, *you* may be the best conferencing partner.

   After the student has read his/her work to a partner, the partner makes suggestions concerning the comprehensibility of the story, and the author marks in changes. For ease of reading and for making changes, it helps if drafts are written on alternate lines.

2. The second part of the conference will involve a second go-over to check spelling and punctuation. Model the *terms* that you expect students to know. Hang up a colourful *chart* of your expectations for student reference.

Figure 6.4

Students compose a story together and type it directly into the computer. The printed hard copy is easier to read for editing purposes.

Sharing a finished product is an occasion for praise and celebrating the author's diligence and efforts. The exact manner of sharing the work can vary: bulletin boards, newsletters, student-made books, reading to another class or group or putting the work on a tape-recorder for the class library. In Chapter 7, "Student Publishing," I share ideas on how to develop student authoring.

Not all written pieces, however, have to go through all the stages of the writing process and not every story draft should end up as a finished, "show" product. Students should have some choice as to which pieces are for show.

Primary students can go through a modified version of process writing. Instead of calling it "conferencing," you could ask them to, "Read your work to a friend to get suggestions for how the story might be made even better."

Figure 6.5

Thematic Learning is often associated with Integrated Language Learning. Subject areas and skills are readily linked in thematic planning. Following a theme allows students to become immersed in a topic, and to follow their interests while using and re-using language to build communication skills and knowledge of the material.

Some Suggested Integrated Language Lessons

In Integrated Language lessons, we, as teachers, must always be mindful of wrapping the four language skills of listening, speaking, reading and writing around a chosen topic or reading selection. It becomes difficult to name a particular lesson as strictly a "reading" lesson because all language skills are used, and each skill is an important component of that learning process. Remember that language, further learning and literacy are viewed in Integrated Language Learning as a continuously interacting phenomenon. This intertwining serves to complement, support and nurture the child in his or her attempts to gain meaning, fuller understanding and retention of a topic.

Once we as teachers become attuned to ensuring that interaction, the next step is to develop a repertoire of strategies to use. When we are not tied to basal readers, then we can capitalize on any topic or theme that motivates children. We can construct an integrated language and literacy event from any number of sources, e.g., a storybook, an incident on the playground, a newspaper article, current events, a children's magazine, a photograph or poster, a caterpillar, a trip, a new ESL student, etc.

The StoryTheme technique (Botel, Booth 1987) that follows can be effectively used in Integrated Language Learning programming. The basic idea is easily adaptable to other materials and topics.

A Sample Language Lesson

In his StoryTheme approach, Morton Botel, an American educator, suggests we start with a *theme* from within a story. For example, before teaching Aesop's fable "Belling the Cat," Botel identified "fear" as an important theme in the fable. To begin, he had his students *identify* instances of fear in their own lives. After *sharing* their personal experiences of fear with a partner, students *wrote* their version of fear. Students found this writing easy to do because they had just practised telling their version and, therefore, had already framed their thoughts.

A large group *discussion* about the different experiences and kinds of fear led to the introduction of "Belling the Cat," a *story* of mice dealing with their historic enemy, the cat. Botel then began to read the story aloud. At a key point in the story, when a major decision was to be made, Botel stopped reading. Student interest was piqued. Botel elicited suggestions regarding possible solutions to the cat problem. He then asked students to take sides in a debate on the merits of two of the solutions suggested. Finally, he read on to the end. Students followed the reading by choosing a variety of literacy activities.

For a similar example of this technique, see *Drama Words* by David Booth (1987).

STORYTHEME TECHNIQUE

- **Identify** the theme of a story or article, e.g., fear.
- **Connections** are made by having students **verbalize** what this theme means from their own experiences, first with a partner and then in small groups (prior knowledge extended).
- Students are asked to record their versions in **writing**.
- **Sharing** a variety of these experiences in a large group then broadens the students' **understanding** of the topic.
- **Read** the story aloud, perhaps stopping at a key point for student **involvement** or decision making.
- Students become involved with a choice of follow-up activities that promote **skills development** in literacy, language, reflection, problem solving and creativity.

Creating an Integrated Language Unit—Books First

Books First is basically a simple twist on an old theme. In the past, whenever we planned for a thematic unit, we have tended to ask the librarian to compile pertinent reading materials at the required levels. Then we set up a display table with as many references and storybooks as possible on that topic.

With the Books First method, we may use the same books as we did in the past, but the students will work in response to the content of the books, as each one is introduced and read by the teacher. In other words, the books are not just a centre to which students might go in support of a theme. *The books become the central component of the theme* and the resulting activities revolve directly around issues and student interests born out of the book's content/storyline. ESL students will benefit from talking with peers about the book and from all the follow-up activities that flow from the students' interactions with that book. The learning choices then become integrated because students have had experience with the text or story, verbally.

BOOKS FIRST GUIDELINES
- Decide on a theme, e.g., Winter, Prejudice, Folk Tales, the Environment.
- Choose a variety of books and articles that will support this theme and that will have meaning for your students.
- Prepare some activities ahead that will help you to meet your own objectives for literacy skills and the concepts you want to develop throughout the theme.

    For example, the book *You Look Ridiculous* was chosen to go with a "Me" theme. In the art centre, students used construction paper to create their own versions of an animal who envied other animals' characteristics. In another group, students relistened to a tape of the story. Some students chose instead to rewrite the original story using people as the main characters. Additionally, students practised making compliments for each member of the class, while yet another group sought answers to the problem of how to alleviate hurt feelings.

- Read one of the books to the class. After you read each book, encourage your students to suggest different activities they might like to do as a result of the reading, so that they will have ownership and choice in their learning, e.g., "What kinds of ideas does this book give you?" "What happened in the story that you would like to try?"
- Introduce the activities you have planned at this time, too.
- After each reading, make the book available, accompanied, if possible, by a tape to support weak readers.
- Each day, choose another book to read to the class and plan new activities with the students. Develop your theme by increasing the complexity of concepts to be learned through books you choose. Student interest will be maintained by the new activities resulting from each new book.

In both the StoryTheme Technique and the Books First Technique, writing ideas down becomes easier for ESL students because language is modelled during discussions about the book. Response journals, expressive writing, reading, art, drama, movies and field trips occur in an integrated fashion.

Related skills and concepts are developed in a "holistic" (therefore meaningful) and a participatory (therefore active) program.

Figure 6.6 (page 64), which summarizes Botel's suggestions for surrounding reading with talking, listening and writing, illustrates how language acquisition, further learning, and literacy combine in Integrated Language Learning.

SURROUNDING READING WITH TALKING, LISTENING AND WRITING

BEFORE READING

Questioning (teacher and/or students) and Discussing
using prior knowledge, textual clues (title, headings, summary, etc.)

Brainstorming
using textual clues
using topic of article
using key words or concepts
using an analogy or problem

Extended Brainstorming + Categorizing + Mapping
using material from text, topic, key words, etc., charting, diagramming, and other visual or graphic representations

Previewing the Text
examining clues to overall structure
setting purposes and general questions
selecting appropriate reading strategies
teacher/student reading aloud

Writing
non-stop: focused or generalized
jotting or note-making
questions
pretest or questionnaire

Enacting
role-playing, improvisation, dramatization, debate, etc.

Constructing
sketching, drawing, building

Viewing
film, video, etc., on topic of reading (while writing)

DURING READING

Teacher-Directed
questioning/predicting
role-taking
playing, doubting/believing
reading aloud

Students Independently
marking or glossing of duplicates of text pages
taking notes
writing questions
partner reading
keeping reading journal

AFTER READING

Discussions
retellings (from different points of view)
responding to any before or during reading activities

Enactments
debate, panel discussion, dramatization, simulation, role-playing, etc.

Oral Presentations
demonstrations; talks

Writing
nonstop: focused or generalized
note-making
writing or answering questions
mapping or revising map
literary or informational text response
making up test

Reading
related material
rereading text from different perspectives

Constructing
sketching
drawing

Viewing
slides, filmstrip, video, film, etc., related to text

Figure 6.6

Suggestions for Surrounding Reading With Talking, Listening, and Writing. Derived from JoAnn Tuttle Seaver and Morton Botel. **Literacy Network Handbook: Reading, Writing and Oral Communication Across the Curriculum**. © *Morton Botel and JoAnn Seaver, 36 Foxglove Road, Levittown, PA, 19056, USA.*

Student Publishing

Reading and writing often culminate in student "published" material. This chapter is devoted to sharing practical ideas, materials and resources for "authoring." It is important that ESL students, indeed all students, have daily experiences with writing. This chapter will also suggest book formats that provide opportunities for ESL students to learn about different styles and purposes for writing. In other words, ESL students will be guided to discover and pattern different kinds of language, e.g., patterning the format of a science Big Book or creating an imaginative story, attempting poetry, rap or a rhyming story, preparing an alternative solution to a story problem or ending to a story, writing in the personal style of individual experiences, or explaining one of their special cultural celebrations. Student authoring can, in fact, create many occasions for cultural sharing.

The suggestions included are meant to support you as you guide your ESL students

- to recognize different styles and purposes for writing;
- in their acquisition of the more formal literate-type of language found in writing;

and

- in the development of their literacy skills.

If you are uncomfortable with an ESL student's "published" work that has errors, you may want to indicate on the title page that this student is a second-language learner.

CAUTION: Primary children who have just started writing are not yet ready for revising. Your evaluation of their "published product" should reflect an understanding of this early cognitive level and focus instead on the process they underwent.

A very important aspect of Integrated Language Learning classrooms is that books are chosen that **initiate a desire in students to respond** to the literature. The students will want to talk about the story and to add to the story from their own experiences and ideas. Publishing capitalizes on this student interest and builds on it. Bookmaking develops student decision-making, organization and sequence skills, creativity, reflection and self-esteem.

Making a book can be a long, involved process and it is only right that students should be praised for their diligence and efforts. To this end, an additional component of "celebrating" student authorship might be added to your plans when the publishing is completed, e.g., reading the book to another class or to the principal, a special sticker, the addition of a page for teacher or peer comments, etc.

Choosing books for your program that have *high student interest* is especially important for second-language learners. Include books that

- have clear pictures, terrific visuals or humour;
- catch the students' interest with the plotline;
- provide appealing language, e.g., rhythm, rhyme or pattern;
- reflect your students' cultures or add a multicultural aspect;
- add a new dimension, e.g., different formats, shapes, creativity;
- contribute to your current themes or other subject areas.

Different Types of Books

I have found it helpful to chart the list of book types on page 67 in large bold letters and display it on a class bulletin board. I add new book types to the list as I find them or as someone draws my attention to a new type.

Figure 7.1

Different Types of Books

- Pattern Books—always acknowledge the original book and author.
- Accordion Books.
- Double Accordion Books.
- Puppet Books—socks through a hole in the book.
- Shape Books—Science related or holiday themes.
- Book-in-a-Box.
- The Story Box—See Figure 7.2.
- Character on the Move Book—main character is on a ribbon.
- Choose Your Own Adventure Books—create different endings.
- Book with Tape—students do the reading and add sound effects.
- Lift the Flap Books—mathematics, riddles, prepositions, jokes or thematic questions with answers under flaps.
- Big Books—photos and drawings of class trips, science projects or individual student patterns of a story.
- Little Books—diaries, telephone books, autographs, A-B-C books, etc.
- Wallpaper Books—blank pages for diaries, presents, memo pads—see Blackline Master #9.
- Pop-up Books—Triangle Pop-Ups, Cage Pop-ups, Arm Pop-ups.
- Dual Language Books—students prepare a book in their first language; an English version is included.

Figure 7.2

The Story Box: The Language Stretcher—ESL students will get lots of language practice when they create and retell their stories using The Story Box.

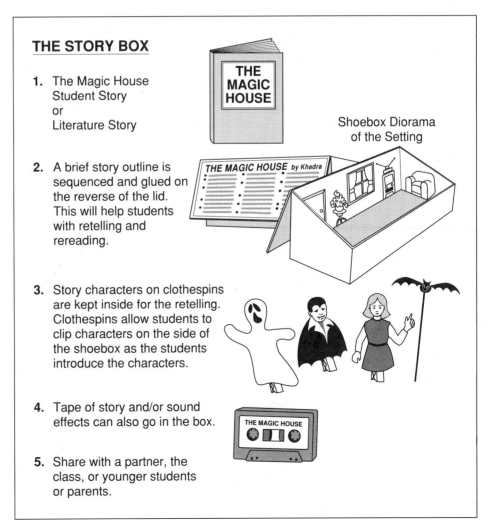

THE STORY BOX

1. The Magic House Student Story or Literature Story

2. A brief story outline is sequenced and glued on the reverse of the lid. This will help students with retelling and rereading.

3. Story characters on clothespins are kept inside for the retelling. Clothespins allow students to clip characters on the side of the shoebox as the students introduce the characters.

4. Tape of story and/or sound effects can also go in the box.

5. Share with a partner, the class, or younger students or parents.

Shoebox Diorama of the Setting

Student Publishing

Before starting on student publishing, you may want to look over the following components to see whether you may want to pursue any of them.

- A Writing Centre with a bulletin board to display suggestions, reminders of the writing process, techniques and/or formats. A visual reminder for ESL students.
- Specially trained student editors or "Editor of the Week."
- A Conferencing Booth or Editor's Desk for peer support.
- A display of "Different Types of Books" as an impetus to vary book formats.
- Space to celebrate students' published work, e.g., table, bulletin board, etc.
- Cross-grade tutoring for editing or illustrating assistance.
- "Book-sharing" (to your class, another class, in library time).
- An arts focus on illustrating techniques.
- Ordering of support materials and audio-visuals.
- Special guest visits by consultants, authors, storytellers and/or illustrators who can add their area of expertise.
- Special trips that enhance student ideas for stories.
- Petition for extra funds to augment your plans, e.g., a school spiral-binding machine, a laminating machine.
- Addition of a class computer(s) for word-processing.
- Inclusion of other languages and subject areas, e.g., books in the first languages, science project books, song books.

Figure 7.3
Bookmaking

Setting the Scene

You may want to try some of the following to get your students started.

1. An introductory session entitled, "Different Types of Books."

    Enlist the help of your librarian to locate a large variety of different types of books, such as are listed on page 67 and shown in Figure 7.1. Show each book to the children and encourage comments.

    Students may have a similar book at home or may have enjoyed reading that particular book. Students could make a list of the different kinds of books in their journals for future reference. Another student could write the types on a chart with a suitable picture for posting.

2. Make a display table of different types of books. Invite students to make themselves familiar with the different kinds, decide which type they would like to try and, if possible, bring in similar books from their own collections at home. Ask for books in the students' first languages at this time.

3. Order kits or reference material that describes the steps involved in bookmaking. Some kits will include filmstrips with a tape that clearly describe the many steps involved in the production of real books. These kits are often available from library departments.

4. Invite a storyteller, author, illustrator or publisher to talk with your students. Seat the ESL students close to the speaker so they can benefit from the gestures and visuals connected with the language. Take time to have new concepts and vocabulary clarified or translated.

    The library and reading department of your school board has sources and contacts that often provide guest speakers. In addition, publishers sometimes look for an elementary level audience to test new material. You might offer your class.

5. Gather a large selection of books that show different illustrating techniques. Ask students to look the illustrations over and choose a technique that appeals to them. Have the students explain what it is about the artwork that they like. Draw students attention to backgrounds and the variety of placements of the print and illustrations. Figure 7.4 illustrates a number of ways the students could vary the layout of their books. You could make up a class survey activity related to book illustrations that would encourage ESL students to use the new vocabulary.

6. Ask someone from your school board's art department to come and share his or her expertise with your students. The representative might also bring in samples from the board's multicultural collections to show a variety of illustrating techniques. You will have to book guests well in advance. Figure 7.5 (page 71) provides some suggestions of how to make a hundred different book illustrations.

7. A piece of sage advice—don't teach pop-up books first. It may be all that students want to do.

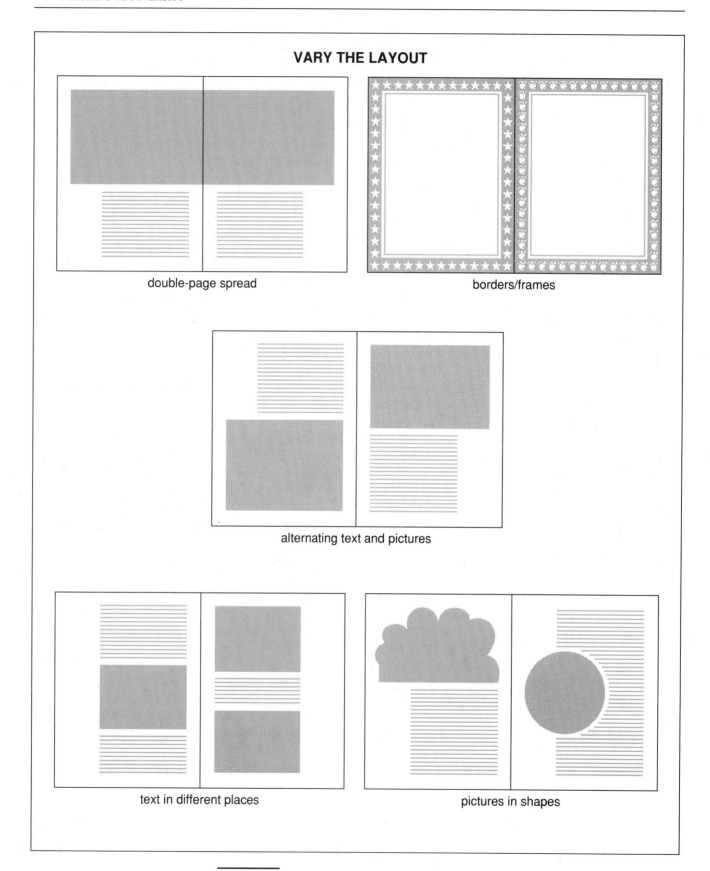

Figure 7.4

You may want to remind your students that they can add interest to their books by varying the placement of text and illustrations on their pages.

Figure 7.5

Illustrations and Backgrounds: Using a variety of special effects arts materials for illustrations, book posters or book covers is a real motivator for students to learn new vocabulary, interact with peers and express their creative strengths.

HOW TO MAKE A HUNDRED DIFFERENT BOOK ILLUSTRATIONS

1. Make your story characters from a material in List 1.
2. Add your characters to a background technique from List 2

For example: textured bear stickers on a green splatter background; felt marker characters against a wash backdrop.

List 1	**List 2**
pictures from magazines	wet paper paint wash
felt markers	splatter painting
students' photographs	marble painting
drawings	dry brush painting
commercial stamps	fingerpainting
silhouettes	Crayola marker with water
stickers	Styrofoam border prints
stencil people and animals	straw blow paintings
children's wallpaper books	sponge painted background
computer graphics	coffee or tea stained
gummed shapes	wallpaper backgrounds
cut or torn paper	glue on tissue paper squares
fingerprint characters	rubbings

I have provided a number of Blackline Masters you may want to use with your students during the bookmaking process:

- #6 Before I Make My Book;
- #7 Book Publishing;
- #8 Sample Dedication and Comments from Readers' Pages;

and

- #9 How To Make Your Own Wallpaper Book.

8 Cooperative Learning

Cooperative Learning combines talk skills and Active Learning. It structures talk around content, requiring that students develop improved skills in thinking, and in language, in order to explain, persuade, encourage, disagree, inform, discuss, and negotiate. It provides ideal opportunities for second-language learners to hear and practise English beyond social language.

Cooperative Learning refers to methods of structuring lessons to ensure that students learn collaboratively, within a support system made up of other students. Initially, we, as teachers, may have to guide students through the development of the social, group and language skills that are necessary to ensure that each child is nurtured in his/her group learning. In a Cooperative Learning system, ESL students benefit from the support and encouragement of other members of their work group. They are encouraged to give information as they are able, and to share their strengths and talents. An additional benefit of such a system to ESL students is the vast amount of peer speech they hear, which provides needed models for language appropriate to any given task. ESL students will hear repeated use of the new vocabulary and grammatical structures in meaningful situations.

Evidence from numerous studies shows that Cooperative Learning improves student attitudes and behaviours towards diversity, boosts self-esteem and improves race-relations among students (Kagan 1985, Slavin's work (1983) as reported in ERIC 1987, Aronson 1978). A special bonus for teachers is that the use of Cooperative Learning structures actually results in rather amazing academic gains—especially for minority and low-achieving students (ERIC 1987).

Collaborations may be as simple as peer-partnering or informal groupings for projects or drama tasks. Taken to a fine art, collaboration may also mean the incorporation of Cooperative Learning as a major organizing principle of instruction. Since students are motivated to learn through listening, speaking, reading and writing cooperatively in small groups or with partners, Cooperative Learning activities are usually Integrated Language Learning activities (Chapter 6), as well.

Figure 8.1

Cooperative Learning is structured so that all students, including ESL students, are required to talk on task and be active participants in lessons, alongside their peers. It is really Active Learning par excellence. Cooperative skills and the language necessary to fulfil them are discussed, modelled and practised as an integral part of the curriculum. ESL students learn appropriate ways of questioning, clarifying, and directing people.

Many excellent resource books are now available to help us, as teachers, to develop Cooperative lessons in all subject areas. It would be worthwhile to initiate a Teacher's Professional Book section in your school library that would allow easy access to good Cooperative Learning reference books at both the primary and junior level.

The intent of this chapter is to pique your interest in developing, or in further developing, your skills in Cooperative teaching. I will provide only a few basic structures, techniques and some strategies that you may find helpful. There are also workshops each year that you can attend and there are professional networks you can tap into to further develop your skills in Cooperative group learning. Certainly, I have found the results of tapping into these resources to be well worth the effort!

Principles of Cooperative Learning

1. **Cooperative tasks are structured so that no one individual can complete the learning task alone.**
   An example: The Jigsaw technique—Each student in the group is required to contribute their specialized work and knowledge of a subsection to a whole topic.
2. **Positive interdependence is fostered and developed.**
   Evaluation is comprised of individual *and* group marks. A reward structure is built in to encourage peer tutoring and support for weaker students in a group.
3. **Students work in different teams.**
   Teams can be of three types: interest groups, random selection or heterogeneous teams. In my classes, I have found using a variety of groupings to be the most effective method. I allow pupils to choose peer-friendship-partners for quick, informal pairings, and concentrate on forming

Figure 8.2

Traditional emphasis on individual/competitive efforts is at variance with the philosophy and structure of Cooperative Learning teams. "...the above [graphic] shows four individuals, listening and talking. The sum of their interaction produces more than if they had worked alone." (Kagan 1988, p. 21)

mixed teams for longer assignments in language arts, projects, etc. Heterogeneous teams are those that include a mix of boys and girls, high and low achievers, outspoken and quiet students, different ethnicity, language levels and behaviours.

4. **Students learn both social and language skills necessary for cooperation at the same time as they learn content/concepts.**

Most cooperative classrooms are made—not chanced upon. When we plan for Cooperation, it means we must first present activities that help students build a team spirit and second, we must identify the behaviours and language for them that will frame mutual support. (See Example 2, page 75.)

Setting the Stage for Cooperative Learning

Example 1

Pat, a Grade 5 teacher in a school with 85% ESL students, has a great, mutually supportive class—every year. How does she do this? No matter what the makeup of her class (i.e., no matter how wide a range of skills, language levels and students with behavioural problems), Pat's class always exudes this noticeable sense of mutual support and cooperation. After visiting her class several times, I recorded the following observations and impressions:

- Students were all busy in groups doing a variety of tasks, chatting, writing, conferring, drawing, constructing, reading books. The pace was very relaxed. Children were laughing as well as talking.
- There was *not* a lot of movement around the classroom. Students were on task. A few were standing behind chairs, looking on or giving advice. Most were sitting casually, draped around papers, books or leaning in towards one another. Occasionally, someone would go get some material or check what another group was doing, but most of the time, the students were very intent on their own business.
- Pat occasionally answered their few queries with a direction to refer back to class routines or group consensus. Pat generally made the rounds of groups, offering advice, praising something and enjoying the children. Only once did Pat direct a raised voice towards a student whose actions were beginning to distract others.

- One time when a student came to her frustrated with something, Pat threw up her hands dramatically and said in a loud voice, "Won't somebody help him? Why doesn't somebody help him?" Several students came right up and off they all went, heads together in conversation.

It was very clear that in this classroom, students knew:

- **Learning is a social act—we work better together.**
- **We all need help at various times—even the teacher.**
- **Encouragement and support for one another are a must.**

When Pat was asked what conscious activities she planned in order to build this kind of cooperation among typical Grade 5 students, she quickly replied, "It's just as easy to be positive as negative, and then you can get something done instead of wasting time." Pat indicated to the class that it was *their responsibility* to maintain the equilibrium.

Whole-class discussions became the venue for planning and problem solving in her class. Pat said, "We did a lot of talking together—in partners and in groups. Honesty and humour, that's the basis."

Example 2

In September, a teacher in a multi-ethnic classroom, who had training in ESL and who was excited at the claims of her first short course on Cooperative Learning, began to incorporate some of the ideas into her Grade 4 classroom. She started by getting her students thinking about cooperation.

Students were directed to do an activity in groups. A full-class discussion followed in which the teacher led the students to identify the problems they had encountered during their group work. Most of the concerns that students raised were directed at certain peer behaviours that either distracted from the task or did not contribute to getting the task done.

Each problem the students identified was written on large chart paper and posted around the room. The groups were then reassigned to discuss and write down their solutions for each problem. They were to concentrate on two things: "What could you *do* to stop the unwanted behaviour?" and "What could you *say* to change that behaviour?"

Back in big group once again, solutions were shared. A selection of several solutions and handy quotes was listed under each of the problems. The students wrote these ideas on the charts themselves. The large, bright charts with student handwriting were displayed for the entire first school term and during parent conferences.

When a student later complained about someone who was not taking turns during group work, the teacher referred the student back to the solutions on the charts.

In this activity, the children were led

- **to recognize which problems might affect their work;**
- **to realize that they could do and say something to alleviate the problems;**
- **to identify the behaviours and language necessary to work cooperatively;**

and

- **to understand that they are responsible to one another and for the work.**

Teambuilding

Students who are going to work together need a chance to get to know one another. Sometimes called "warm-ups," these bonding activities fulfil two important functions, especially for reticent ESL students:

- They introduce and acquaint the students with one another.
- They develop a sense of team identity required for future collaboration.

To ensure maximum participation, groups or teams should include four to six students. Varying the teams allows the students opportunities to form a variety of social relationships. Every time a new team is formed, there should be new "teambuilding" activities, and at the end of the team's time together, there should be some team-leaving activities as well. Ideas for team-leaving activities are at the end of this chapter.

Some Suggested Activities for Building a Team

Brainstorm   To find three commonalities among the group members (Teams find three differences, three favourites things, etc.)
Rules for brainstorming are

- go for speed;
- accept all ideas, no matter how silly they may seem;
- don't evaluate the ideas now;
- build on other people's suggestions (synergy).

Line Ups   In each team, students line up in order of their heights, birthdays, alphabetical order, etc. This activity could be followed up with graphs.

Name Adjectives   Team members write their names vertically on pieces of paper. Other members help think of positive adjectives or phrases that start with those letters and describe that person.

Group Task   To complete a quiz or puzzle, brain teaser, or word search.

Assembly Line   Usually a craft project. Each student does one thing, then passes it on to another student, e.g., in mural building, one student paints the background, another draws the pictures, another cuts them out, another glues them on and another writes the labels, etc.

Interviews   Partners interview each other and then introduce each other to the rest of their team. Topics could include favourite food, music, holidays, movies, books, sports, etc.

Team Name   Teams come up with their own name, handshake, logo, crest, secret greeting or chant. A consensus activity to establish team identity.

Arts Project   Team members create a mobile of members' names and interests; build a structure with toothpicks or rolled newspapers; develop a mural together, etc.

Team Problem Solving   Team members reach a consensus in activities such as "Lost on the Moon" and "Shipwreck and Survival on a Desert Island." In both these games, the team must agree which seven objects would be the most useful to retrieve from the ship, before it leaves or is sunk.

Cooperative Learning Structures

I have found the following group strategies to be particularly effective in fostering and encouraging Cooperative Learning. They are also easy to use.

1. Brainstorming   Can be done in any subject
   • to find a solution to school litter, or a story character's dilemma;
   • to suggest cause-and-effect relationships (if trees grew dollars instead of leaves...);
   • to decide on a class trip or fund-raising project.

2. Think-Pair-Share   Everybody gets a say.
   • The teacher asks a question of the whole group.
   • Everybody has time to think of his/her own answer.
   • Students then pair up and discuss their answers.
   • After a signal for silence, students have a chance to share their ideas with the whole group.

3. Twos to Fours   It's in the retelling.
   • Students pair off to do an activity or solve a problem.
   • Two sets of partners then join to share their ideas again.

4. Numbered Heads   Speak on behalf of the team.
   • Students number themselves from one to four.
   • The teacher then asks a question for discussion, e.g.,"What do you think...?" or "Why would...?" or "How would you...?" Try to frame questions that elicit discussion about the students' current studies.
   • Students talk together in their groups to contribute to a team answer.
   • After the silent signal is given, the teacher calls out a number. Only those students designated by that number will raise their hands to respond. For example, teacher calls out number 2. Student #2 in every team raises his/her hand to answer.

Figure 8.3

Research findings indicate that boys tend to dominate groups while girls tend to exhibit supporting behaviours. Using Listening Triads, Talking Chips, Critical Friends, or Role Cards helps to resolve this problem. The Jigsaw technique also requires that girls contribute as much as boys. (Oracy Project. 1991. **Teaching, Talking and Learning in Key Stage Three**. *Great Britain: National Curriculum Council Enterprises Ltd., p. 20)*

Figure 8.4

In "Think-Pair-Share" and "Twos to Fours," students learn content better by hearing ideas from others and by retelling, rethinking and rephrasing their own thoughts. ESL students, in particular, need this cyclical approach to language use.

5. Listening Triads   Everybody is a specialist.
   • In groups of three, students take on the roles of talker, questioner, or recorder.
   • The talker explains or comments on a brief task.
   • The questioner prompts and clarifies.
   • The recorder takes notes and reports for the group.
   • Next time, the students change roles.

6. Critical Friends   Watch what you're doing!
   One team member is chosen to observe how the team works together. This observer, using a guide such as in Figure 8.5 (Blackline Master #10), watches and listens as his/her team works. *It is best in this activity to focus on one social skill at a time. As this skill is discussed in class and observed within their own groups, students will internalize that skill for use in future tasks and behaviours.* After the activity, the observer shares the information with the team. The ensuing discussion helps children think about their individual work styles as well as their group effort.

Focus on developing group awareness of one social skill at a time. As this skill is discussed and observed, students will internalize it in their group behaviours. Within a short while, students will have incorporated a range of desired cooperative group skills.

---

7. Role Cards   I've got a job to do.
   • Each team member is given a card with a special role to carry out during group activity, e.g., Timekeeper, Recorder, Encourager, Summarizer, Praiser, etc.

Figure 8.5

*Sample Student Group
Observation Sheet*

Task <u>Trip Fundraising</u>

Date <u>Oct. '93</u>

Group Members	Contributed Ideas	Listened to Others	STAYED ON TOPIC new skill*
Ali	✓	sometimes	✓
Mezghan	no-really shy	✓	?
Mohamed	talks too much	not really	✓
Annahita	✓	sometimes	No-
Joyce	✓	✓	✓

COMMENTS

We have a good group but Mohamed is too bossy and Mezghan is too quiet. We got to finish faster. Joyce is a good speller so she should be the note-taker.

<u>Amir</u>
Signature

*Takes turns, shares materials, stays on task, asks questions, summarizes ideas, helps others, etc.

8. **Talking Chips**   Take turns.
   • Everybody on the team receives three or four tokens.
   • Each time a member contributes an idea, he/she must put one of the tokens into a pile. When all of his/her tokens are gone, the student cannot offer any more ideas until all the other people in the group have finished their tokens, too. The tokens can then be redistributed.

Roving Reporters (Spies or Envoys) are a unique twist. Each team chooses a member to travel around to other groups, listen in and bring back more ideas to the team. This technique is best saved until teams are almost "thought out."

---

9. **Round Robin**   I'm next.
   • Students take turns giving an answer or adding an idea.
   • Regularly used as a story-building technique, round robin can also be used for recalling a story sequence, reviewing the times tables, writing a silly story, creating lists, adding to a picture, etc.

10. **Jigsaw**   Also called Expert Groups
    Jigsaw is a four-step structure.

    Step one   Students form a "home" group.
    Step two   Each student is assigned a number, colour or letter. The topic overview is presented.

Step three Students now move to form an "expert group" with other students who have same number or colour, etc. Each "expert group" works on one part of the larger topic.

Step four When time is up, the experts regroup with their original home groups. Each expert now teaches the skills or content learned in his/her subtopic to the home group.

- All members contribute something to the topic, so everybody is an expert.
- Team members depend on one another to complete the overall task.
- Each team member must learn skills or content from the others.
- Evaluation depends on both an individual mark and a team effort mark.

AN EXAMPLE OF A COOPERATIVE JIGSAW

A Grade 4 teacher had his class study the fairy tale genre in language arts and multicultural education.

Figure 8.6

What Happens During a Cooperative Jigsaw Activity

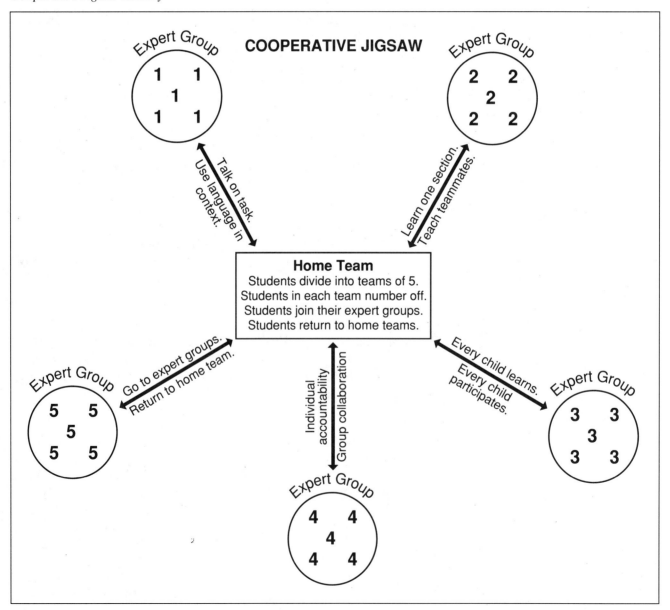

This teacher chose five stories from the countries of origin of the students. The overall task was for the students to read one of the fairy tales and practise telling it with a view to sharing that story with their teammates. The lesson sequence that the teacher followed is outlined below.

- Students in a home group of five numbered themselves off.
- Students moved from their home groups to their expert groups where they studied the same fairy tale. After they had read and practised the tale together, the students returned to their home groups.
- Students told their tales to their teammates over the next several lessons. Each story was related to the genre.
- Students responded to the task and discussions in a response journal.

Evaluation and Recognition of Group Work

Evaluation of group work should include a strong emphasis on the growth and improvement of cooperative skills. For this reason, most reference books include team evaluation forms of one sort or another. Figure 8.5 (page 79) is an example of one observation sheet; it is reproduced as Blackline Master #10. Such forms will help identify for students which skills are important. They also indicate to students that growth in cooperative skills is going to be evaluated along with a finished product.

After any teamwork has been completed, group members need to talk about their development in cooperative skills in order to internalize what the members did well and to identify what they need to improve. This oral processing provides us as teachers with ideal opportunities for formative evaluation. Team evaluation forms completed by each member should be kept as a record of progress and for reporting to parents.

Recognition of efforts and finished products can take many forms. Consideration should be given to rewarding individual improvements as well as group success and whole-class progress. Recognition and rewards can be as simple as giving a compliment or class applause to providing special stickers, a treat, extra computer time or first choice for an activity, etc.

Taking Leave of the Old Teams

Activities to acquaint students with one another and to build team spirit are essential to ensure bonding, a requisite for cooperation in future work. Just as necessary are team-leaving activities.

Members of teams that are disbanded suddenly, with little thought to the relationships that students have developed during their work together, will probably experience difficulty when regrouping into new teams. It is essential to ease students out of the old teams and into the new. Some of the best team-leaving or parting activities are from Spencer Kagan (1988,1986). In using the following activities, Kagan, a leading authority on Cooperative Learning, prepares students for team changes in a positive way.

1. Take a snapshot of teams well before they part and have the photos posted, or have the teams paste them in the class scrapbook.

2. Have the teammates make a final statement to the class as a team—"What we have learned together."

3. Have teammates introduce one another to the class as exciting potential new teammates. "What you can really learn from (student's name) is..." "One thing you will like about working with (student's name) is..."

4. Have students write a parting letter to each of their teammates, emphasizing, "What I have learned from you," and/or "What I have enjoyed about working with you." More sophisticated students can deal with regrets as well as appreciations, for example, "If we had more time to work together, I would like to..."

What To Do When They Arrive Brand New

Throughout the day we as teachers want to feel that our lessons are successful. To this end, there must be a feeling first, that children are learning, at whatever level they can grasp concepts and content, and second, that students are happy while carrying out their tasks.

Each of these criteria on its own will not give us complete satisfaction. If a lesson is learned but the students let it be known that they were unhappy about the tasks, then we need to rethink how to present the material in a more palatable form. If the material itself is not learned, then we need to consider alternative steps to ensure comprehension.

A non-English speaking student who cannot learn through conventional methods and who looks extremely uneasy in class is bound to make a conscientious teacher uncomfortable. Teacher's Colleges, in general, have not prepared us for what to do when students "arrive brand new." Therefore, in this chapter I deal with the basics—ours and theirs. After a little preliminary pedagogy, I offer some practical suggestions that are designed to include the non-English-speaking student in regular programming, activities that I have found effective with my ESL students. In addition, I offer suggestions that I hope will assist you in providing individual and small group activities at the new ESL student's level. At the end of the chapter, I provide a "Beginning Materials List" suggesting a number of materials that can be used successfully with new ESL students.

There are specific strategies suggested from research and practice that can make the teaching and learning of second languages easier and more effective. In Blackline Masters #1 to #3, I have synthesized much of this research into chart form that you can use to help you program for your ESL students. I originally designed these masters as self-checking, self-confirming strategy lists for teachers who wish to evaluate their own program and, at the same time, gain further guidance as to directions, methods and ideas to try next. Blackline Master #1, "Atmosphere," provides an overall philosophy to guide your integration of ESL students. Blackline Masters #2 and 3, "Program" and "Interactions," provide more specific suggestions for successful integration.

Figure 9.1

The first thing to remember is that the newcomer is fearful of many things: you, the other children, expectations, routines and his or her own inability to communicate. Having a ready smile and a lot of empathy is an excellent start to building future bonds of respect, cooperation and achievement.

Beginning speakers of English are said to be **at a Basic level of fluency**. However, some ESL students may have studied English in their homelands and so their English literacy skills may be substantially better than their English verbal fluency. Many times the program of English taught in foreign countries is based on the Grammar Translation approach (Chapter 3, page 21) which does not prepare students to communicate verbally.

By necessity, instruction at this Basic English level, that is, for non-English speakers, will be very teacher-directed (or peer-directed) and lessons will focus on building needed vocabulary. *There will not be a lot of give-and-take verbally.* Many new students will even hesitate to repeat words after you. This level of fluency prohibits the student from using vocabulary or structures (grammar) to share thoughts, wishes or other functions of language. Although the student may say some things spontaneously, these utterances will, in all likelihood, be single words or memorized phrases such as "water" or "go washroom." Most newcomers will be fearful of addressing you, but, if pressed, they may speak in soft, shy tones.

In many multi-ethnic schools, certain procedures have been established to help ease children of newly arrived immigrant families into the school.
- Wherever possible, a new student is placed in a class where another student speaks the same first language.
- The ESL teacher is called to meet family members and their translator and to conduct (or arrange for) a school tour. During this time an initial assessment and background information form is filled out (see Figure 9.2). This information is then shared immediately with all the new student's teachers.
- School information (hours, availability of dental care and special days, etc.) and community information (information about adult ESL classes, daycare facilities, ethnic associations, and the Red Cross telephone number) is given to the family. Many schools have this information available in translations.

Some Key Points To Remember

• Find out what the student can do.

Get essential background information on the student's previous level of schooling and exposure to English. Some students will understand a lot more English (receptive ability) than they will be able to show or use (expressive ability). Some students have had a crash course, from a relative or parent, on our Roman script, and still other students may have studied English in their previous school. Often, it is surprising how many key phrases the new student has learned in preparation for school here.

An ESL background information sheet such as in Figure 9.2 will help guide you during initial interviews with the family and the student. Information can be added throughout the year if additional important issues surface. (Figure 9.2 also appears as Blackline Master #4.)

BACKGROUND INFORMATION SHEET

Name _Mohamed O._
Country of Birth _Somalia_
Arrival Date _Dec. 11/92_   Grade _4_
Address _407 Glen Parkway, Apt. 1703_

Date _Jan./93_
Phone _694-7341_
Languages _Somali, French_
Birth Date _4/6/'84_

A. Family Background:

Is family together? _No_   Does anyone in home speak English? _No; however, he has an uncle at_ _483-7962 who can translate. Mother here with 4 children. Father killed by soldiers last_ _year. M. is youngest. Two sisters in Middle school and older brother in high school._

(Add further details on <u>reverse</u> side.) ➡

Languages parents/siblings are literate in _Arabic and Somali_
Health _good_   Talents/Interests _soccer, reading, Nintendo_

B. Previous Schooling:

French school (private) in Djibouti   *Attach reports.* _none_
Reads in the ̶L̶1̶ L2 _French_   Writes in ̶L̶1̶ L2 _French_   *(Ask for student sample and <u>attach</u>.)* ✔
Previous Exposure to English _1 month in holding centre, uncle taught some English words._
Attach math sample. ✔   Approximate Level—Needs _good skills, can multiply by_ _2 digits—simple division_

C. English Proficiency on Arrival   Level _Beginner/Basic_

Verbal Fluency: Can say alphabet ✔   Recognizes letters ✔   Matches caps & small ✔
Can write alphabet ✔   Knows phonics ✔

Use a picture file to elicit student responses for the following:

Colours ✔   Basic Verbs _No_   Prepositions _No_   School Vocabulary _No_
Can talk about a picture in—single words/phrases/sentences *(Circle one.)* _No_
Comprehends—simple directions ✔ , a story _No_
Counts up to _12_   Recognizes numbers ✔   *Attach math sample.* ✔
English Literacy: English reading level _N/A_ Writes in English _N/A_ *(Attach sample.)*
Assessed by _M. Meyers_   Date _Jan. 93_

D. Conference/Monitoring Follow-ups *(Attach any pertinent information.)*

Date _May.93_   Comments _excellent progress in all areas, spontaneous speech in English._
Date _____   Comments

Figure 9.2
Sample Background Information Sheet for a newly arriving ESL Student

• Teach frequently used vocabulary first.
(See also "Best Beginning Topics for Basic Level ESL Students" on page 87.)

What are the *essential words* an ESL student requires in order to get started? Try school vocabulary: pencil, book, eraser, recess, come, go out, etc. Also teach colours, days, easy opposites, simple verbs. Build up a collection of drawings or pictures that illustrate these words as well as the "Dolch" reading list of 200 of the most commonly used English reading words. *If the student reads in another language and has prior knowledge of our phonetic system*, the Dolch is a good list to send home for translation as the list provides a basic English reading vocabulary quickly.

• Stress the use of the first-language skills.

When your students write, ESL students should write in their first language if they know how. A student of the same language could translate. Allow the new student to do project work in his/her first language. Students can often obtain information on projects or for homework from home sources. If a student can read in another language, then send a buddy with him or her to obtain library books in that language so the child can read when others read. Otherwise, ensure that a good selection of children's picture books and magazines with lots of illustrations are on hand for the ESL student's use during class reading time. I often see new non-English-speaking students, who can't read English, pouring over books at our reading corner.

• Use student translators in teaching content areas.

Just because the student can't put an English word to a concept doesn't mean the child can't learn the concept in his or her own language. Establish a buddy system whereby peers who speak the same language share in the "teaching-translating" of the new student.

• Usually, you should speak in single words, phrases or short, simple sentences when addressing the non-English-speaking child directly.

If you use regular sentence length and speed the student will hear only an "*acoustic blur*"—he/she won't be able to distinguish or hear when one word ends and another starts. Accompany your instructions with gestures and visuals to aid meaning. Students can easily learn chunks of language through rote memorization: "How are you?" "That's mine." "Water, please?"

• Introduce a reading word with the spoken word.

Have the new words written, illustrated with a drawing and, if possible, translated into the first language as well. I often send a list of new vocabulary home to be translated and call it homework. However, if a student has no or little literacy in his or her first language, then before sending vocabulary home to practise as a reading assignment, I make sure the student has basic alphabet skills such as saying by rote, recognizing and knowing the letter names, matching capitals and small letters, and having an awareness of English phonics.

• Take 5.

Using a student translator for even five minutes can go a long way to ensure your newcomer knows

- what the class and school routines are;
- what's going on, e.g., current task or theme;
- what he or she should study at home;
- what trips or special days are coming up.

• Every student goes through a "Silent Period."

While they are coming to grips with expectations and "testing the waters" many students are silent. Accept this behaviour but be warm and encouraging. *This silent period can last many months.* If there is a buddy who speaks the same language, notice whether the child is conversing freely with his/her new friend. You will feel more at ease when the new student shows signs of typical social speech behaviours even if they are in the first language.

• Best Beginning Topics for Basic Level ESL Students

Consider what language the Basic level or beginning ESL student needs to use immediately.

During the first several days, the student will need

- words for school objects and places
- people titles and names, e.g., librarian is Ms. _____
- time words and numbers, e.g., recess, 10:30
- alphabet—names, sequence, matching
- survival phrases—washroom please, My name is..., my telephone # is ....
- numbers and colours

During the first month, the student will need

- days of the week
- months of the year
- mathematical terms
- basic opposites, e.g., up - down, yes - no, mother - father, in - out, girl - boy, come - go, big - little, etc.
- family words, e.g., mother, father, sister, grandfather
- basic verbs—run, come, stand, write, read, count, etc.
- prepositions—in, on, under, beside, behind, etc.
- weather words and seasons
- time and money, including first, second, third, etc.
- any vocabulary specific to your class theme
- words for special days or events, e.g., Hallowe'en, Sports Day, photo day.
- clothing and body words

It is not expedient to teach vocabulary as discrete items as in the above list nor to teach the list in sequence. For one thing, the student may not wait until week #2 to learn the days of the week, especially if the class is going on a trip three days hence. *Language should be learned when and where it is most meaningful.* For example, in the Math timeslot, which includes activity centres and teacher-directed lessons, the Basic level student could be learning colours, numbers, and students' names while helping to prepare a graph of the other students' hair and eye colour.

In other words, teach vocabulary that allows the student to get on with his/her learning and encourage the Basic level student to mix as much as possible with that student's best resource—his or her peers.

Some Activities for Basic-level Second-language Learners

While many of the following activities are also useful to native English-speaking Canadians, they are particularly effective with beginning ESL students.

• Language Experience

Reading and writing that results from a shared experience is a powerful tool for assisting students acquiring English. This process is called the **Language Experience Approach.**

It is easy for ESL students to relate language spoken in meaningful, natural ways to the printed symbols. For example, the first Spring flower is brought in to class and the children automatically talk about colour, size and smell. Better yet, bring in a flower that has not yet blossomed. Have the children discuss the future bloom, draw a picture of what it might look like, share those pictures in a big group and then compose a chart story. This is a particularly good activity for the ESL student if the chart also includes visuals and colours alongside short sentences.

Students then take turns reading the sentences after the teacher models them. Later, the chart story is reread and particular content words are highlighted for review. The chart is posted. The highlighted vocabulary could be written on cards to be made into games, e.g., Concentration, bingo, word-matching.

Eliciting language from a student's artwork and paintings follows this format as well. However, the important oral input from peers is usually missing from this type of individual activity.

The sequence of Language Experience is

1. **experience (or activity)**
2. **oral expression**
3. **reading and writing**
4. **review and consolidation (re-using and games)**

It should be noted that ESL students can gain as much at their level during these activities as native speakers who are consolidating their reading and writing skills through language-experience activities. This natural integration of oral speech with listening, reading and writing provides a quality language lesson for everyone.

Your Best Bets

Best Resources—Use of Visuals (drawings, graphs, photos, diagrams, maps, charts)

Best Reading Approach—Language Experience Approach

Best Writing Approach—Language Experience Approach

Best Help—A first-language translator or buddy

Best Materials—Big Books, bingos, crafts, trips

Best Reading Support—A Reading Partners Program

Best Topics—High Need and High Frequency Vocabulary

• Books, Books, Books

When you have a limited budget and little time to prepare, then grab your favourite storybooks. A story that is told with verve, that includes visuals and that can be simplified or rephrased for ESL students can also be the beginning of a great lesson. For example, *The Gingerbread Man* story can be used successfully even with junior level students if you choose activities in chanting, patterning, puppetry, drama, baking, and fractions for a gingerbread recipe.

Also, choose books that relate to your themes or curricular objectives. Remember that ESL students should be exposed to language that is slightly above their spoken or expressive ability. Vocabulary can be modified or an alternative word quickly juxtaposed, as you read, without diminishing the experience.

It is natural for ESL students to understand more language (receptive ability) than they can actually speak (expressive ability).

Big Books are even better. Whether they consist of favourite literature stories, a compilation of catchy rhymes and poems, or junior level science topics, Big Books focus children's attention. They usually have large, clear, charming visuals that directly relate the meaning to the printed word. You can point to each word or phrase as the selection is read a second time, which helps ESL students focus on the printed word and learn the English convention of reading from left to right on the page. The script of some other languages, unlike English, goes from right to left or bottom to top. In addition, many Big Books have accompanying smaller books with a tape for pleasure reading or to support weak readers. ESL students benefit from repeated readings by the teacher, by assistants, by other students, or on tape.

Figure 9.3

• Homemade Bingos

Your class could help make a variety of different bingo sets.

While bingo provides a fun way to practise new reading vocabulary for your English-speaking students, it also helps teach needed vocabulary to the ESL students. It allows the newcomer to hear repeated use of the new vocabulary—in single words, then phrases or short sentences. When most of the items are known, the newcomer can take a turn being the bingo caller and in this way practise pronunciation with peers providing positive reinforcement.

Bingos should include a matching label (word) for each picture. Although the number of vocabulary items in the whole bingo can be numerous, it is a good idea to place only ten to fifteen pictures on any one card. Not only can a large number of items on one card be rather overwhelming, but there is a strong possibility that the game might not get finished in the time allotted.

Handy bingo sets to have on hand include school words, animals, colours, basic verbs, food, opposites, prepositions, and seasonal, thematic and curriculum topic vocabulary.

Space out the pictures and matching words and paste them onto cards made of brightly coloured Bristol board. (Old primary dictionaries make excellent sources for bingo pictures.) Laminate the cards for longer wear. Store them in a decorated shoebox or baggie. Different coloured bingo chips are available at most department stores.

• Crafts

Crafts and art activities are fabulous techniques for teaching and reinforcing vocabulary and language usage. All children need multiple opportunities to experiment with new materials, manipulate different media and express themselves through creative activities. Crafts and art also provide perfect vehicles for including Basic level second-language students within regular programs.

Teaching vocabulary in drills isolated from real language use is like teaching someone to swim on land. Let's look at an example to show the difference between book-type learning and real language use. In order to teach the English name of body parts, there are many dittos on which students can label the parts or fill in the blanks. There are also lots of patterned exercises where students repeat a sentence and substitute a different body part, e.g., "This is my nose," "This is my mouth," "This is my _____."

In contrast, a teacher was overseeing students who were working on a Spring activity about planting. This day's activity had the students covering a soup can with paper and then decorating it with eyes, nose, hands and feet, etc. The finished can was filled with soil to receive the grass seeds which grew into lovely, long, bright green hair. The major body parts were learned in the context of a craft that supported the overall topic of Spring. The learning in this case was meaningful and fun. *Legs* had to be bent so "Hairy" could sit down. *Arms* were folded up to wave at passersby. Several children gave their can-people *haircuts*. Body parts were reviewed again through more crafts, songs, measurement activities and skits about visits to the doctor.

There are many craft books that offer a wealth of activities that can be adapted to support various language lessons and themes for ESL students. In fact, it is a good idea to seek these out whenever planning for a variety of multi-sensory and manipulative activities for any theme you plan.

• Reading Partners Program

No matter what the grade level or how formal the arrangements, a reading partnership between two students is beneficial to all concerned.

The partnership boosts the self-esteem and leadership qualities of the one who does the helping; it offers valuable assistance in the way of language, kinship and skills development to the student receiving the support; and it relieves the teacher to know the ESL child is receiving a form of individual help.

Reading partners can be an informal arrangement within a class and with peers within this class or it can involve cross-grade exchanges on special topics. Whatever the assortment of pairings you decide to use, there are several points to consider ahead of time that will help ensure success.

- Assist or confer about the selections that will be read and shared. If the materials are well chosen and at the appropriate level they will maximize the benefits of the partnerships. Otherwise, both students may become dissatisfied, one because the material is boring or incomprehensible, the other because the partner seems inattentive and restless.
- Do you want the students to focus on an aspect of the reading that can be a stepping stone to writing? For example, when a Basic level student had finished several readings of *I Can Play*, he was asked to compose his own version of an "I can play _____ " booklet.
- Meeting with the reading helpers for half an hour ahead of time will allow you to create the proper tone for the partnerships, state your expectations for quality assistance, and discuss strategies and alternatives should the partnership run into difficulties. Ensure that students know you wish to be informed of successes and problems on an ongoing basis.
- Have the partner materials accessible. Place them in large, decorated, envelopes with names so everybody can get straight to business.
- A group sharing time is worthwhile. It encourages students to try out the new ideas and materials as shared by other partners.

Figure 9.4

Reading partners boost self-esteem and language for both students

• If you are partnering within your own class, start out with a class discussion that focuses on the need for the students' input and support. If you are partnering with another grade, then start out with a specified time—say once a week for the duration of a theme. Evaluate this experience with your students before trying it again.

• What's Missing?

Sit in a circle and place four to six items on the table or floor. You might use different coloured crayons, a variety of school objects, plastic fruit or animals. Have the students try to repeat the names of the items as you point to each. Mime hiding one behind your back and then showing it. Ask the students to close their eyes while you hide one again. You may have to repeat the direction, "Close your eyes" while passing your hand over the ESL children's eyelids. When you are ready, say, "Open your eyes." You may have to repeat this on the first several tries but the students will pick up the idea quickly. Point to the empty space where the object was and say with a shrug, "What's missing?"

Praise the student who correctly states which object is missing and immediately show it while repeating the word that identifies the object.

After several times, let the ESL students take turns choosing an object to hide. Your non-ESL students can play this with ESL students for up to ten minutes.

• Cube Toss (A five-minute lesson)

This game is useful for a quick drill on any thematic vocabulary. It involves making or buying a cube frame (also available from Math departments). The best size is 9 cm x 9 cm. If you can obtain a pre-made form, it is a good idea to use tape and acetate to make little see-through pockets on each face. Then you can re-use the cube for a variety of purposes as you slip in the new pictures or words, e.g., school objects, alphabet letters, verbs, weather words, etc.

Figure 9.5

What's missing? Here, three students have their eyes closed, while the other student, encouraged by the teacher, removes one of the items from the collection on the table.

Figure 9.6

You point to each face of the cube and say the new words. **The cube is then rolled on a table or the floor.** Students call out the word for the picture that faces up. The first student to call out the correct word then gets a chance to roll the cube for others. Small groups are recommended so that everybody gets a turn. Students tend to get a little noisy in their excitement.

When introducing new vocabulary, choose a reasonable number of new words. Although fast-paced drills are standard ESL techniques, try to get the students to use the new words in a game format that will keep their motivation high.

• Alphabet Activities

While many newcomers have some knowledge of the alphabet, many others find our Roman script to be a totally new phenomenon. The following alphabet activities will help students in this situation.

ALPHABET POCKET BOARD

This handy, fold-up alphabet board has been used over and over again in my room. You can make one quickly with sturdy poster board. Label library pockets with capital letters and then attach them to the board in sequence. A final pocket can be used to hold the cards when they are not in use. Print small letters on separate cards which can then be inserted into the corresponding "capital" pocket, with the small letters showing.

Stand the alphabet board on the floor with a small group or with a single student sitting in front. Start with all the small cards inside their matching capital pocket. While the students are watching, pull out several letters that are obvious matches, e.g., the small c, j, k, m, o, p, s, u, v, w, x, z. Hand one of the cards to a child and then indicate by pointing to the board that you wish the letter to be returned to the appropriate pocket (Figure 9.7). When this is done correctly praise the child, showing that this is the correct procedure for this activity. Then

Figure 9.7

Figure 9.8

Sample Alphabet Tracking Sheet

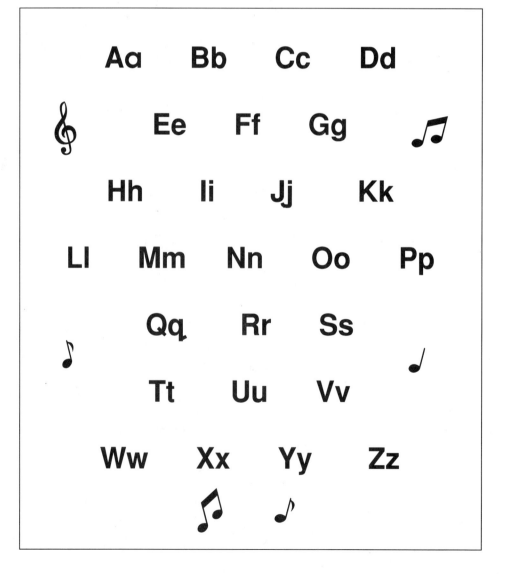

distribute the remaining cards and after saying the letter name, have the students replace them. You could play this several times and shuffle the cards before distributing them. Have the students take the cards back to their seats to practise writing those letters.

On another day, show students the alphabet tracking sheet (Figure 9.8) attached to the back of the board. Then pull out several small letters that *do not have the same configuration* as the capital letter. Go for student success by not using too many new letters all at once. Students will have to get up and down as they learn first to locate the small letter on the tracking sheet and then to return to the front of the board to place the letter in the right pocket. Incorrect placements are easy to spot as the small letter cards stick out over the top of the pocket. Figure 9.8 has been reproduced as Blackline Master #11.

Library pockets can also be used to match words that the student is learning to the appropriate picture cards. Other students might use a similar idea for retrieving high-frequency spelling words to copy while writing stories and journals.

Pocket layouts also work well on a door or on a small bulletin board.

SAYING THE ALPHABET

Sing out the alphabet with students every day, while pointing to each letter. Alternatively, chant it, rap it, have students echo the letters back. Another student/volunteer should sit with the ESL child and *verbalize* when the child is doing an alphabet puzzle or "stamping" out the letters in sequence on paper. I am always a little suspicious of "silent" activities with this level of ESL student.

MATCHING AND SEQUENCING

Have students work with a peer tutor or within a small play group to complete these activities. *Given multiple opportunities*, these activities will familiarize the ESL student with the names and sounds of our English alphabet.

- Bingo. Teacher-made or commercial alphabet bingo.
- Feel and Tell letters made from sandpaper, cut out and mounted on cards. Students reach into a bag, choose one of the letters and say its name. If they don't know the letter's name, pull it out so everybody can name it.
- Computer programs. Most programs comprise several games of matching and sequencing the letters. Some computer programs will even talk to the students.
- Card games for matching, e.g., game of concentration, B - B or B - b. Also, students place 8 x 11 letter cards along an alphabet "clothesline."
- Students use Plasticene "worms" to make the letters in their names.
- Puzzles.
- Commercial foam letters. Students *paint* out the sequence on long strips of paper. (Cash register rolls are good.)
- Cut-and-paste certain letters from magazines.
- Alphabet stamps (and ink pads) in both capital and lower case letters.
- Magnetic letters for sequencing on the chalkboard.

LETTER FORMATION

Students unfamiliar with our alphabet must be shown how to form the letters correctly. *Don't assume* they will learn how to write the letters correctly by osmosis. It's best to set aside several lessons to teach or review letter formation soon after the students' arrival. Many ESL students will need direction on the spacing of letters, too. While primary students usually do printing lessons on one or two letters at a time, older ESL students can be shown as follows:

- letters formed from o—a, o, b, d, g, p, q;
- letters with tails—g, j, p, q, y;
- tall letters—h, t, l, d, f, k;
- capitals and matching small letters.

Most commercial alphabet books have tracing and forming and sequencing activities that can be used for homework review.

INITIAL CONSONANTS (PHONICS)

If ESL students have been allowed many opportunities to hear and play with the previous alphabet activities, then most of those students will have a basic background to begin to relate to sound-letter correspondence tasks. Teacher-led lessons *that elicit **known** vocabulary* and illustrate one letter sound at a time enable ESL students to learn phonics very quickly. Student-created collages of pictures for one letter sound, either hand-drawn or cut from catalogues and magazines, are far superior to using a commercial phonics ditto book that contains lots of unknown vocabulary items.

Figure 9.9

• The Language Master

The language master is a machine that talks to students. Students can also be taught to use the recording device. Envelopes of different categories of words (animals, alphabet, verbs, prepositions) are prepared with a picture and word on the special language master cards. The students will need a two-minute lesson on how to put the cards through the machine to listen (Figure 9.9). Thereafter, it is a student-run activity. You will have to make up the sets of cards with the vocabulary you wish the students to review.

You can also prepare cards to help both ESL and native English-speaking children with their reading and math skills. There is one particularly useful suggestion in the handbook *Learning With Magnetic Card Activities*, which makes use of a stop-gap device so students can make a guess and then push the card through to verify their answer.

• Student-Made Books

Reading and writing are easy to learn when the material is tied directly to the student's current interests and activities. That's why student-made books are a good follow-up to a lesson. Books needn't be a long production. If you have lots of ready-cut papers (8 1/2 x 11 is too big) then students can avail themselves of bookmaking at any time with just a stapler.

A Polaroid camera is great for bookmaking. Take photos of school personnel and special rooms in the school. Discuss these, name them, put them in sequence and glue them onto coloured construction paper with a label. The Polaroid Company often will send a representative out to your school for a workshop loaded with great ideas *for all your students*, plus a special discount on a class camera.

The simplest book can be "My"—e.g., my pencil, my book, my mother, etc. Allow the students to volunteer their ideas and pattern previous answers. You'll be surprised at how much vocabulary they do know.

One book that resulted from a lesson with new ESL students was, "Come." An experience chart was developed first, with the students contributing to the pattern. For seatwork the students were asked to complete a book that would go home for practice. The book read, "Come here, Come to the gym, Come to the table, Come to my house," etc. Each page was numbered and included a picture.

There are easy pattern books galore that allow you to follow up on this activity in your own classroom.

• What's in the Bag?

As an alternative to a boring language drill, this is a fast-paced guessing game for vocabulary review that all students enjoy. Use a bag that is not too flimsy and that students can't see through. Put in an object from a topic your ESL students are learning. Once I used a stuffed white seal toy when we were studying zoo animals. In Spring, I used a plant, at Hallowe'en, a candle. As soon as my students see me holding up and shaking the bag they call out, "What's in the bag?" You can ask the question generally or have students take turns to guess. You might encourage students with greater language fluency to ask simple questions or you might offer a hint. Sometimes, you could have students stick their arms in the bag and feel the object. We've done a version of this game with textured alphabet letters too. We usually write a short version of that day's game on a group chart to copy.

• Music Activities

The love of music is universal. Students in all cultures have grown up with parents' little chants, rhymes and songs. Music, then, is transcultural—across cultures. Musical activities complement an Integrated Language Learning program (Chapter 6) because music encompasses a variety of skills—listening, speaking, singing, creating, movement, vocabulary development, reading and writing.

The appeal of the rhyme, intonation, rhythm and patterns of music provides an easy means for students to acquire English for speaking and reading purposes. One reading program is even called *Chime-In* (Jean Mallock).

The addition of hand and body movements, sound effects and instruments to accompany songs contributes to easier retention for most students. Basic level second-language students will respond during this type of group activity at their own level and without fear of ridicule.

Singing lets children play with language.

A simple, repetitive song increases students' awareness of English sentence structure. You can then capitalize on this awareness to encourage the students to pattern their own verses. Popular children's singer Raffi has a series of songbooks that are bright, multicultural and melodic, e.g., *Everything Grows*. If you write a very popular song or verse on a chart in large, clear letters, the verse can serve as a reading lesson as well. Claude Belanger's Big Books and tapes (e.g., *I Like the Rain, My Dog*) are favourites in many classrooms because the Big Book visuals are great and the songs are rhythmic and fun.

Musical activities may include the use of lummi sticks, dance and free movement, Orff and band instruments, recorders, Chinese ribbons, the parachute, chants and echoes, listening centres and choirs.

Figure 9.10

A happy song about friendship and getting along is made more meaningful to this mixed Grade 1 and 2 class by the addition of a handshake for each chorus.

• Computers

Teaching a Basic level second-language student how to use a computer program is a good lesson in itself. Try to number simple steps as you mime the procedure of loading the disc and turning on both the screen and computer console.

- One—Load the disc.
- Two—Turn on the screen.
- Three—Turn on the console.

Once that is done, there are many excellent programs that can support language learning in a variety of subjects. Obtain programs for reinforcing alphabet matching and sequence in games, simple counting, addition and subtraction, multiplication and division, money, time, measurement, etc.

The wonderful new *Discus Books* programs are probably a little too advanced for the beginning level ESL student but a few months down the line, those high Basic level students would enjoy being read to by a computer with sound effects. Computer networking—writing to someone in a different school on the computer and receiving notes from that person—is also a great idea, but this activity is for students with the ability to compose.

There are now keyboards available that write in other languages, with a non-Roman script. You may eventually be able to get one for your school.

• Field Trips

Outdoor education is a wonderful way to acculturalize ESL students to their new country while developing communication skills. Seasonal trips to a ravine, woodlot or farm will allow you to plan many lessons—to prepare students with vocabulary for what they'll see and after, as follow-ups in speaking, writing, reading, viewing (video/photos), art and drama.

The students' excitement of experiencing something new and worthwhile will make your task easier as you introduce classroom activities that develop and enrich students' language. When students are taken outside once again, they will go with an increased sense of wonder and language facility to share in further learning.

Initially, outdoor trips *should* allow children the freedom to behave naturally—to run, to shout, to explore, to discover, to investigate and to follow their natural inclination to find out about their world. It is in this way that ESL students will learn the vocabulary and sentence structures of their peers and, in turn, lose some of their timidity, get caught up in the excitement and start to verbalize.

These outdoor trips early in the year also help students to *bond*, with the result that classroom activities will show greater collaboration and verbalizing.

Figure 9.11

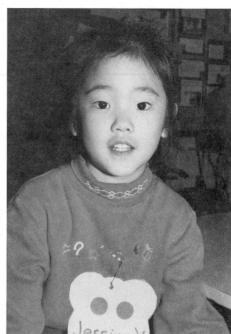

Beginning Materials List for Basic Level ESL Students

I have found the materials listed below to be particularly effective with my beginning ESL students. Use, adapt and build on this list for your Basic level ESL students.

- Alphabet Pocket Stand—with removable cards.
- Basic Vocabulary Builder—available from Teacher's Discovery, 1-800-521-3897; great source for pictures and card games.
- Bingo sets—animals, verbs, clothing—cut, pasted and laminated on Bristol board.
- *Bridge Reading Program* by A. Dewsbury—visual, universal themes, a "bridge" to reading, OISE Press.
- *Book Bank*, 30 starter books, Scholastic Publishers.
- *Canadian Picture Dictionary*—great pictures, large print, multicultural, Houghton-Mifflin Publishers.
- *Can You Do This*? boxed book sets by Developmental Learning Materials, *I Can Swim, I Can Play*, etc.
- Claude Belanger Big Books and Sing-Together tapes—Shortland Publications.
- Computer Programs—check with your board of education's computer department for a listing, description and cost.
- *Creature Features*—Big and little books—one of eight from *Share It!* Series, Nelson Canada.
- *Crossword Puzzles for Beginners*—reproducible, thematic, Editions Publ. Inc., Welland, Ontario.
- Cube Toss for vocabulary game—cube forms often available from packaging stores for use with new vocabulary.
- *Expressways 2*—Level 1—*Skip Along*, Gage Educational Publishing Company.
- *Fairytales, Folktales and Fables: Literature-based Projects*, Creative Teaching Press, Inc.
- Great Beginnings—a binder of thematic units from the Toronto Board of Education.
- *Hats Hats Hats*—by Ann Morris, Lothrop, Lee and Shepard Books.
- *Impressions—How I Wonder, When the Wind Blows*, available as student readers and as Big Books, choral reading and chiming-in, Holt, Rinehart and Winston of Canada.
- *Instant Language Builders*, short text, long text and no text available—Developmental Learning Materials.
- *I Know an Old Lady Who Swallowed a Fly*—puppets, book, movie, song.
- *I Was Walking Down the Road*—Big Book and little books, Scholastic Publishers.
- Language Master Cards and Machine—available from Ontario Learning Concepts.
- *Literature Activities for Young Children Book 3*—(reproducible), Teacher Created Materials, Inc.

- New Student Assessment Form (see Blackline Master #4).
- Outdoor Trips—to parks and ravines. Automatically creates the desire to speak and share the excitement and wonder of discovery. Students can verbalize freely when outdoors and learn from peer speech.
- Categorized Picture Card Sets—multiple uses; some come with teacher's guide.
- Picture Cards for Dolch and high frequency words, teacher-made, wall charts, etc.
- *Pumpkin Pumpkin*—Big Book, Scholastic Publishers.
- Raffi—*Everything Grows*—Book and tape—several others in the series, Crown Publishers.
- Ravensburger Puzzles—Match-a-Balloon (colours) and Opposites.
- Sequencing Cards—heavy-board cards in 3, 4, 6 or 8 story-card length, most teacher stores.
- Spell-a-Puzzle, Jumbo floor alphabet, number and colour puzzles (large pieces).
- *STEP Into Reading*—'86 easy readers, Level 1, Random House.
- *Storybox Series*—primary books, Ginn Publishers.
- *Storytime*, Early Learning Activities, Jean Warren Publishing House, Inc.
- *Sunshine Books*—primary, Ginn Publishers.
- *The You and Me Series*, Big Books and little readers, Nelson Canada.
- Toba Hoban books—great pictures, easy to follow up with student-made books, Greenwillow.
- Toy Unit—teacher-made materials and idea builder—an alternative to a Christian religious Christmas Theme.
- Unicorn—reader series—*One by One* and *Sing a Rainbow*, McGraw-Hill Ryerson Publishers.
- Variety of student-made books—school staff and rooms, my ____ , colours, etc.
- Verbs, Verbs, Verbs—each large card in this set includes visuals for eight different ways to use a verb, Pippin Publishers. Multiple uses.
- What We Do Day by Day—Poster Cards, National Dairy Council, USA.
- *Who Uses This?*—by Margaret Miller, Greenwillow Books.
- School board movies—choose a variety of non-verbal and simple storylines as well as versions of children's favourites and seasonal Disney films.

10 Education for a Global Perspective

M any futuristic movies depict an urbane, economic and technological elite that governs ragged, often brutish masses. The elite are uniformly white, but the masses always comprise mixed races, occasionally punctuated by bizarre alien creatures.

Many of us would react with dismay should it be brought to our attention that these fantasies are not unlike the reality of our present-day elites, and, of course, our schools. Yet we don't really have to look at a science fiction movie to see the similarities.

The Los Angeles riots of 1992, the Oka crisis in Quebec in 1990, issues of police brutality in Montreal, Toronto and Vancouver, Stephen Lewis' 1992 Report on Race Relations in Ontario, Spike Lee's *Malcolm X* movie—all of these and more have refocused North American attention on critical issues of race, poverty and inequity.

Governments have stated their intentions to deal more actively and effectively with racism and inequity, whose manifestations are poverty, discrimination, distrust and disorder in society. At the elementary school level, however, we do not have to wait for governments to act. We have within ourselves the resources to act, if only we have the will. Education for a Global Perspective should be viewed as an entry point for addressing these societal ills.

Education for a Global Perspective subsumes Multicultural, Intercultural and Anti-Racist Education. However you name it, in essence, the goals of Education for a Global Perspective must include

- developing student respect for the culture and values of other ethnic groups as well as for their own;
- helping students appreciate human similarities as well as differences;
- providing opportunities for students to experience peoples of different ethnicity and countries in positive and mutually supportive ways;
- demonstrating active efforts to understand and redress issues of intolerance and racism;
- nurturing in students the ability to problem solve, to assess perspectives and information and to seek honesty and justice.

Figure 10.1

Multicultural Education

"It has been said that without a culture we cannot see, but with a culture we are forever blind. In other words, each of us is born into a culture that teaches us a number of shared meanings and expectations. We usually learn our own culture's way of doing, speaking, and thinking so well that it becomes difficult to think, feel and act as people in other cultures do....Using our own culture as the standard by which we judge other cultures is called ethnocentrism." (Irving 1986)

The term "multiculturalism" means many things to different people. Some critics feel strongly that multiculturalism implies merely tolerance, rather than ensuring that minority group citizens are involved in their own empowerment. Some see multiculturalism as cooperation among ethnic groups for the enrichment of all, while others view it as the rejection of common goals and the rise of group self-interest and preservation.

Arthur Schlesinger, Jr., an influential American author, refers to multiculturalism as "the tribalization of American life" and equates it with "separatist pressures" (*TIME* Magazine, July 8, 1991). Unfortunately, in our classrooms, many well-meaning attempts to program with a multicultural focus have tended to celebrate the differences among peoples rather than emphasizing the empowerment of minority groups within our society. This interpretation of Multicultural Education has helped to create a superficial "tourist-style curriculum"—i.e., the 3 F's of multiculturalism: the Food, Festivals and Famous People of an ethnic group. Figure 10.2 describes the dangers of addressing multicultural goals in such a way.

Schlesinger represents those who see multiculturalism as **divisive**, as "rejecting integration." Advocates of multiculturalism see it as **inclusive**. They see multiculturalism as an opportunity for minority peoples finally to enter the mainstream of Canadian society as empowered individuals, secure to offer their

Figure 10.2

CAUTION

WARNING: TOURIST CURRICULUM IS HAZARDOUS TO THE DEVELOPMENT OF YOUR CHILDREN.

Watch out for the signs of tourist curriculum:

Trivializing: Organizing activities only around holidays or around food. Only involving parents for holiday and cooking activities.

Tokenism: One Black doll amid many White dolls; a bulletin board of "ethnic" images—the only diversity in the room; only one book about any cultural group.

Disconnecting cultural diversity from daily classroom life: Reading books about children of colour only on special occasions. Teaching a unit on a different culture and then never seeing that culture again.

Stereotyping: Images of Native Canadians all from the past; people of colour always shown as poor; people from cultures outside Canada only shown in "traditional" dress and in rural settings.

Misrepresenting Canadian ethnic groups: Pictures and books about Iran to teach about Muslim Canadians; of Japan to teach about Japanese-Canadians; of Africa to teach about Black Canadians.

Adapted from Louise Derman Sparks and the A.B.C. Task Force. 1989. *Anti-Bias Curriculum.* Washington, DC: National Association for the Education of Young Children.

---

talents and skills, unobstructed, and free of the emotional and economic burdens associated with racial and ethnic oppression.

Those of us who view multiculturalism in this way envision Multicultural Education as the vehicle that gives minority students the freedom to access a quality education that empowers them

- in their language and literacy attempts;
- in their appreciation of themselves and of their heritage;
- in their respect for the rights and freedoms of others

all within the context of being Canadians (Meyers 1988).

Figure 10.3

"Flight for Freedom,"
Canada Post Corporation's
Canada Literacy Symbol

Intercultural Education

In fact, many teachers have recognized the importance of integrating Multicultural Education into the ongoing curriculum, rather than treating it as a separate subject. What these teachers ask for, however, is more guidance, more materials and more information on how to do this. Moreover, with limited funding, some teachers have felt that no money meant no materials, and consequently, they couldn't "do" Multicultural Education. There is now, however, a new way of thinking about what we do and how we use the resources available to us in classrooms.

An *Inter*cultural focus provides a uniquely different approach to teaching about diversity. As an educational perspective, students are taught to look for the similarities, or universalities, among humans and then to develop an appreciation for diversity by looking at the reasons for differences. That is, Intercultural Education connotes an emphasis on the similarities of human needs and an active seeking to understand the rationale for differences, not simply the celebration of those differences. Intercultural Education thus subsumes Multicultural Education.

Example

A Nutrition Theme with an Intercultural Focus would not only include foods that students eat in their own homes, but would

- include discussions of how geography, history and weather may have affected the types of food that are available to people;
- direct attention to the concepts of hunger and malnutrition and talk about these issues (problem solve in groups, justice, equity, redress);
- consider gender roles, modes of dining, holiday foods (values, women's issues);
- investigate environmental concerns regarding the use of packaged, processed or fresh foods (global issues);
- look at the resources and contributions of developing countries to the food products that students consume in their homes (interdependence).

Therefore, while examining food as a universal need, students develop an awareness of and investigate the differences in cuisine and conventions and our dependence on the resources of other countries. The actual sharing of foods and customs can still be covered within the scope of this theme, but the students will come to these activities having developed a wider understanding of the rationale for human diversity—they will have a more Global Perspective.

In other words, the best way to prepare students with Education for a Global Perspective is to permeate all curriculum with a willingness to promote student reflection on issues of inequity, racism and redress, as they surface, rather than involving the students in sporadic moments of cultural sharing.

There are a variety of excellent, often inexpensive Global and Intercultural resources that can help us to guide our students to a greater understanding of our interdependence with other peoples and countries. There is a brief listing of some of these resources for curriculum use at the end of this chapter.

An Intercultural or Global perspective can be incorporated into any topic. It does not require large amounts of money or pre-made materials to get underway. What it does require is an inquiry approach with lots of sharing and discussion among the students in class and with their parents.

Anti-Racist Education

Anti-Racist Education tackles problems of identifying, dealing with and redressing those attitudes and behaviours that discriminate against people because of their colour, ethnicity, or religion. Further, Anti-Racist Education supports the inherent dignity, rights and freedoms of all peoples.

It is now widely recognized that racism awareness is intrinsic to Multicultural/Intercultural Education. The United Kingdom's Institute of Race Relations noted that minority groups do not suffer inequity because of their ethnic differences per se, but because those differences are at the lower end of a system of racial hierarchy. The Institute's concern, therefore, became not Multicultural, Multi-Ethnic Education, but Anti-Racist Education, which by its very nature includes the study of other cultures and groups.

In *Moving Into the Mainstream*, Jill Bourne describes British efforts to develop better programs for minority students. She reports that the most effective programs were found in schools with their own policies for equal opportunities and Anti-Racist Education. In Canada, we already have national, local and school board policies that state the ideals of equal opportunity and multiculturalism. But what appears evident from both research and practice is that in order to ensure effective action, each individual school administration must set its own standards, reflect its own expectations and set its own example for staff and students to live and work in ways that show a belief in and commitment to Anti-Racist Education.

Figure 10.4

Global Education includes issues of racism, human rights, social justice, systematic and historical redress, environmental interdependence and personal responsibility.

- To begin with, Anti-Racist Education means going beyond a review of books and curriculum to ensure an anti-racist focus. It includes updating the curriculum by building in an Intercultural/Multicultural and Global perspective. Global Education usually includes the themes of friendship, cooperation, interdependence and personal enrichment through Intercultural/Multicultural Education. An anti-racist school ensures that its students' realities and cultures are reflected in its curriculum.
- Anti-Racist Education also means that we, as teachers, may need help to understand and identify entrenched prejudices in language and institutions, as well as in our own lives.
- Equally important, we need to develop strategies for tackling the day-to-day issues of racism, powerlessness and poverty: how to resolve racial conflicts, *what to say when attending to racist comments from students or colleagues.* As is the case with Intercultural/Multicultural Education, when we as teachers feel unsure of "how to" and "what to" address vis-à-vis racism, we will not be effective in planning and carrying out related goals.

In short, the task of implementing Anti-Racist Education is everybody's duty—from policy-makers and directors of education right down to resource staff, classroom teachers, secretaries and caretakers in our schools.

Common and complementary goals of Intercultural/Multicultural and Anti-Racist Education serve to link their aims and efforts under the banner of Education for a Global Perspective. Global Education includes issues of racism, human rights, social justice, systematic and historical redress, environmental interdependence and personal responsibility.

"If we [educators] turn our eyes away from the structural inequities in our schools re policies, programs and practices, then we are disempowering ourselves and...if we don't recognize the reality [of diversity], then how can we prepare our students for the global society that will be of the twenty-first century."—Jim Cummins, Plenary Speech, TESL Conference, Toronto, Ontario, November 27, 1992.

What Can We Do To Empower Our Students?

- **Realize that perspectives are different.** "When a teacher attempts to elicit student background experiences in a unit of study, the information from ESL students will probably be 'interculturally packed.' By encouraging ESL students to share their experiences, ideas, and stories teachers are already promoting Interculturalism. Gordon Wells, in an interview I had with him in 1987, said, 'Views are not arbitrary. They are part of the reality the students live in.' *It is in the ways we show acceptance and encouragement of the ESL student's reality in our daily programs, as well as in the school lobbies and hallways, that we can validate student ethnicity.*" (Meyers 1988)
- **Include the heritage languages,** e.g., bulletin board signs in the first languages, bilingual books, translations of important messages home, multilingual libraries, valuing students as translators or parents as helpers
- **Give feedback to people who make derogatory and racist comments as soon as it is appropriate.** "Ensure that expressions of racist sentiments, whether the result of ignorance, thoughtlessness or malicious intent, are not tolerated in the classroom or in the school." (D'Oyley and Shapson 1990, page 31)

At times this feedback must be given right away. Sometimes, however, you may want to meet with the students involved at recess or after school, when they have calmed down and can discuss the issue rationally. When initiating a discussion, tell a student directly when a comment is racist and why it is racist, and that it will not be tolerated in your school. You may want to keep records for certain students who repeatedly display this type of behaviour and bring it to the attention of your administration.

Initiate a class discussion in which a conflict situation is shared with students for their input and solutions. Figure 10.5 shows a form that can be used with your students. It is reproduced as Blackline Master #12. Encourage students to reflect and respond to the discussion personally in journals or some other form.

- **Ask for Professional Development on conflict resolution and peace action groups.** Many of these projects involve resource staff who work with the students themselves.
- **Acknowledge the presence and contributions of persons of different ethnicity:** visible in newspapers and magazines, such as medical researchers, newscasters, TV personalities, business and professional people, journalists, writers, reporters, police, speakers, politicians, etc. Use these sources. Invite visiting artists to provide multicultural resources in arts, drama, music, and literature.

Figure 10.5

Different Points of View:
This form will help students consider different perspectives that people bring to a problem. Initially, students may need to be encouraged to expand on or to explain their reasoning. Soon, however, discussions can concentrate on student reflections and creative thinking.

A.

_____The Wolf_____ **thinks**	_____The 3 Pigs_____ **thinks**
-He is hungry.	-They should have stayed home.
-Pigs taste good to him.	-My brothers are lazy.
-Little pigs are easy to catch.	-Wolves don't eat pigs.
-Nobody can stop him.	-Wolves should eat lambs.
	-We need some help.

B.   **What I Think**

I think the farmer should chase the wolf away or drive him far away and leave him in the woods. The 3 pigs need a house alarm for when the wolf comes.

- **Be a role model.** Students will love it when you try to speak a few words of their language, when you speak up on their behalf, when you welcome their families as sources of information and help, and when you show interest in their cultures.
- **No teacher is expected to become knowledgeable about all cultures.** Rely on your students to share their important cultural traditions. Realize that when you encourage culture-sharing among students, your multi-ethnic resources will increase dramatically.

One teacher regularly encouraged her students to inform the class of upcoming special events. When a cultural event of importance to several students was mentioned, she asked those children, as part of their work, to prepare a short presentation for the rest of the students.

At the end of the week, the ten-minute presentation included a written script explaining the celebration, pictures, and a demonstration of special jewellery and clothes brought from home with the permission of a parent. The other students had an opportunity to ask questions. Some started to relate this new knowledge to things that were similar in their own experiences.

The presentation was so well done that the students took their "show on the road" to share with several other classes in the school. This was also a good example of Integrated Language programming.

Enriching Us All

We learn from, and our lives are enriched by our contacts with other peoples and cultures.

Figure 10.6

Teachers, with the help of their school's resource-librarian, have available to them now a wide selection of storybooks and tales from other countries and cultures. As well, many books originating in North America are finally depicting our multi-ethnicity in their illustrations.

In "Critical Thinking To Reduce Prejudice," Debbie Walsh advises educators to teach children to ask questions, to seek perspectives from all sides and to adjust their thinking accordingly. When students reflect rather than react, when students are led to problem solve and make decisions intelligently, then we will have taught them something far more important than facts. When all is said and done, this is what real teaching is all about. Figure 10.7 is a form that can be used to encourage problem solving in a variety of subject areas. The figure is reproduced as Blackline Master #13.

As we hear through the latest advances in communication about political, economic and environmental concerns, it seems that the farthest reaches of the world are not so very distant after all. We are linked to other nations by such things as trading relationships, concerns over pollutants and the realities of climactic and political upheavals. Changing dynamics in countries create an impact felt throughout the world.

Figure 10.7

Students can use this form for discussions, environmental issues, student-based concerns, story problems, etc. If students are assigned to complete the tasks in small groups, there will be greater discussion and support for the second-language learners in the group.

The Problem
Cinderella's stepmother is mean.
Snow White's stepmother is really mean.
How can we make stepmothers nice again?
Solution #1
Do extra work or make her breakfast.
Solution #2
Tell your father so he can divorce her or something.
Solution #3
Run away. I'd go live with my aunt's family.
I've got lots of cousins to play with there.
Solution #4 Not all stepmothers are awful.
Maybe Cinderella and Snow White were unlucky.
They should have asked somebody for help.
Which solution seems the best to you? Be prepared to say why you chose the solution you did.
Put a red star ★ beside the solution you favour.

Figure 10.8

The topics in this figure were elicited from a Global Education flow chart. All of the topics will provide you with opportunities to guide your students in discussion and investigation towards meeting the goals of Education for a Global Perspective.

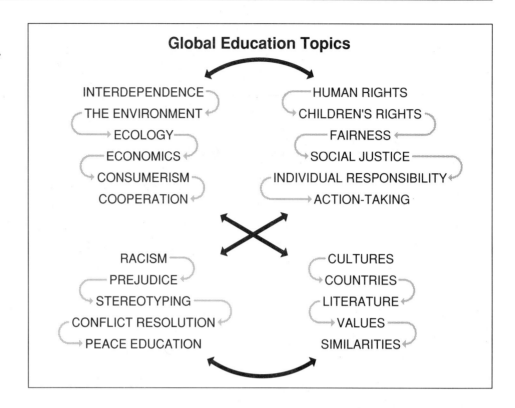

Global Education Topics

INTERDEPENDENCE
THE ENVIRONMENT
ECOLOGY
ECONOMICS
CONSUMERISM
COOPERATION

HUMAN RIGHTS
CHILDREN'S RIGHTS
FAIRNESS
SOCIAL JUSTICE
INDIVIDUAL RESPONSIBILITY
ACTION-TAKING

RACISM
PREJUDICE
STEREOTYPING
CONFLICT RESOLUTION
PEACE EDUCATION

CULTURES
COUNTRIES
LITERATURE
VALUES
SIMILARITIES

Disasters, worldwide, create a cry for both a response and relief from "better off" countries. Increasing attention is drawn to the misuse and abuse of resources in underdeveloped countries by the "overdeveloped" countries. Futurists and environmentalists claim that the destiny of humankind depends on the willingness of world powers to tackle their responsibility for the intelligent planning and sharing of the resources of our planet—to ensure a better life for all of our species. We have been drawn, inexorably, then, towards Global awareness. If humankind is to flourish, we must teach our children to coexist and to cooperate with all the world's citizens.

Teaching, as the training of both mind and character, offers educators myriad opportunities to prepare children to meet this challenge. By adding the dimensions of Anti-Racist, Multicultural and Intercultural teaching, we will go a long way towards providing students with a truly Global Perspective—towards ensuring mutual survival and a better world in the twenty-first century.

Curriculum Resources

Many of the following sources of Intercultural/Multicultural/ Global Education are inexpensive and most have reproducibles.

- Red Cross
- UNICEF
- OXFAM
- *Anti-Bias Curriculum*, Louise Derman Sparks and the A.B.C. Task Force, National Association for the Education of Young Children, Washington, D.C., 1989
- *Children of the World, A Primary Unit*, Alberta Global Education Project, 11010 - 142 Street NW, Edmonton, Alberta, T5N 2R1, 1990, 1-800-232-7208

- *Globalchild, Multicultural Resources for Young Children*, by Maureen Cech, Canadian Cataloguing in Publication Data, Ottawa, 1990
- *Somewhere Today* (free quarterly magazine) Media-Sphere, Youth Editions, P.O. Box 1310, Postal Station B, Hull, Quebec, J8X 3Y1
- *Within Our Reach: Helping Students Develop an International Perspective*, Two separate Resource Units, one for Primary and one for Grades 5 - 8, UNICEF
- *World Cultures: A Theme Guide to K-12 Curricular Resources, Activities, and Processes*, Bay Area Global Education Program (BAGEP), Stanford University Press, 1984
- *Learning the Skills of Peacemaking*, Naomi Drew, Jalmer Press, 1987
- *Start-Up Multiculturalism*, Cindy Bailey, Pembroke Publishers, 1991
- *Our Classroom. We Can Learn Together*. 1983. Moorman, C., and D. Dishon, Englewood Cliffs, NJ: Prentice-Hall Regents
- *Helping Kids Learn Multicultural Concepts: A Handbook of Strategies*, Michael Pasternak, 1979
- Center for Teaching International Relations Publications, University of Denver, 2199 S. University Blvd., Denver, CO 80208, 1-800-967-2847
- Intercultural Development Research Association, 5835 Callaghan Rd., Suite 350, San Antonio, Texas 78228

Bibliography

Aiello, B. (Ed.) 1975. *Making It Work: Practical Ideas for Integrating Exceptional Children into Regular Classes*. Reston, VA: The Council for Exceptional Children.

Allen, Virginia Garibaldi, and Pat Rigg. 1989. *When They Don't All Speak English*. Urbana, IL: National Council of Teachers of English.

Ambert, Alba N. 1988. *Bilingual Education and English as a Second Language: A Research Handbook 1986-1987*. New York, NY: Garland Publishers.

Anderson, B., and R.W. Joels. 1986. *Teaching Reading to Students with Limited English Proficiencies*. Springfield, IL: Charles C. Thomas.

Aronson, E. 1978. *The Jigsaw Classroom*. Beverly Hills, CA: Sage Publications.

Ashworth, M. 1985. *Beyond Methodology: Second Language Teaching and the Community*. New York, NY: Cambridge University Press.

Bailey, Cindy. 1991. *Start-Up Multiculturalism*. Markham, ON: Pembroke Publishers Limited.

Banks, James. 1987. "Social Studies, Ethnic Diversity, and Social Change." *The Elementary School Journal*. 87:5.

Barton, Bob, and David Booth. 1990. *Stories in the Classroom*. Markham, ON: Pembroke Publishers Limited.

Baskwill, Jane, and Paulette Whitman. 1986. *Whole Language Sourcebook*. Scholastic Publications.

Bay Area Global Education Program. 1983. *Teaching World Literature in the Global Classroom: A Theme Guide to K-12 Curriculum Resources. Activities and Processes*. Stanford, CA: Stanford University Press.

Birckbichler, D.W. 1987. "Classroom Materials for Second Language Proficiency." *Theory Into Practice*. 26(4):294-300.

Blackhurst, A.E. 1982. "Competencies for Teaching Mainstreamed Students." *Theory Into Practice*. 21(2):139-143.

Booth, David, W. 1987. *Drama words: the role of drama in language growth*. Toronto, ON: Toronto Board of Education.

Botel, Morton, and JoAnn Tuttle Seaver. *Literacy Network Handbook: Reading, Writing and Oral Communication Across the Curriculum*. Levittown, PA: Morton Botel/JoAnn Seaver.

Bourne, Jill. 1989. *Moving Into the Mainstream:* LEA provision for bilingual pupils. Windsor (Berkshire, Eng.): NFER Nelson.

British Columbia, Ministry of Education. 1987. *English as a Second Language K-12. Resource Book, Vol. 1. Integrating Language and Content Instruction*. Victoria, BC: Ministry of Education.

Brown, H.D. 1987. *Principles of Language Learning and Teaching. 2nd Edition.* Englewood Cliffs, NJ: Prentice-Hall Regents.

Burke, M.A. 1986. "Canada's Immigrant Children." *Canadian Social Trends.* Spring 92:23-27.

California State University, Bilingual Education Office. 1986. *Beyond Language: Social and Cultural Factors in Schooling Language Minority Students.* Los Angeles, CA: Evaluation, Dissemination and Assessment Center.

Cambourne, B. 1987. "What Happens in a Whole Language Classroom." Paper presented at Hong Kong English as a Second Language Conference. Wollongong, N.S.W. Australia.

Cantlon, Teresa L. 1991. *Structuring the Classroom Successfully for Cooperative Team Learning.* Third Edition. Portland, OR: Prestige Publishers.

Chamot, A.U. 1983. "Toward a Functional ESL Curriculum in the Elementary School." *TESOL Quarterly.* 17(3):459-471.

Chamot, Anna Uhl, and J. Michael O'Malley. 1987. "The Cognitive Academic Language Learning Approach: A Bridge to the Mainstream." *TESOL Quarterly.* 21(2):227-249.

Charles, C.M. 1974. *Teacher's Petit Piaget.* Belmont, CA: Fearon-Pitman Publishers Inc.

Cochrane, Orin, Donna Cochrane, Sharen Scalena, and Ethel Buchanan. 1984. *Reading, Writing and Caring.* Winnipeg, MB: Whole Language Consultants Ltd.

Collinson, Vivienne. 1991. "Child-Centred Learning." *FWTAO Newsletter.* 10:3.

Crandall, J. (Ed.) 1987. *ESL Through Content-Area Instruction.* Eaglewood Cliffs, NJ: Prentice-Hall Regents.

Crawford-Lange, Linda M., and Dale L. Lange. 1987. "Integrating Language and Culture: How To Do It." *Theory Into Practice.* 26:4.

Cummins, J. 1986. "Empowering Minority Students: A Framework for Intervention." *Harvard Educational Review.* 56(1):18-36.

Cummins, J. 1984. *Bilingualism and Special Education: Issues in Assessment and Pedagogy.* Clevedon, Avon, England: Multilingual Matters Ltd.

Cummins, J. 1983. "Language Proficiency, Biliteracy and French Immersion." *Canadian Journal of Education.* 8(2):117-138.

Cummins, J. 1981. *Bilingualism and Minority-Language Children.* Toronto, ON: OISE Press.

Cummins, J., and M. Swain. 1986. *Bilingualism in Education: Aspects of Theory, Research and Practice.* New York, NY: Longman.

Curran, Lorna. 1990. *Cooperative Learning Lessons for Little Ones.* San Juan Capistrano, CA: Resources for Teachers, Inc.

De Monchy, Margaret Leiper. 1991. "Recovery and Rebuilding: The Challenge for Refugee Children and Service Providers." In Ahearn, Frederick L., Jr., and Jean L. Athey. (Eds.) *Refugee Children: Theory, Research, and Services.* Baltimore, MD: The Johns Hopkins University Press.

Di Giovanni, A., and M. Danesi. 1988. "The Role of the Mother Tongue in the Development of the Ethnic Child." *Orbit.* 19(2):10-12.

D'Oyley, Vincent, and Stan Shapson. (Eds.) 1990. *Innovative Multicultural Teaching.* Toronto, ON: Kagan and Woo Ltd.

Drew, Naomi. 1987. *Learning the Skills of Peacemaking: An Activity Guide for Elementary-Age Children on Communicating, Cooperating and Resolving.* Rolling Hills Estates, CA: Jalmer Press.

Early, Margaret. 1990. "ESL Beginning Literacy: a content-based approach." *TESL Canada Journal.* V7:2 March.

Early, Margaret, Bernard A. Mohan, and Hugh R. Hooper. 1989. "The Vancouver School Board Language and Content Project." In Esling, John H. (Ed.) *Multicultural Education and Policy: ESL in the 90's.* Toronto, ON: OISE Press.

Educational Research Service. 1991. *Culturally Sensitive Instruction and Student Learning.* Arlington, VI: Educational Research Service.

Edward, Viv, and Angela Redfern. 1992. *The World in a Classroom:* Language in Education in Britain and Canada. Clevedon, Eng./ Philadelphia, PA: Multilingual Matters Ltd.

Elkins, D.P. (Ed.) 1979. *Self-Concept Sourcebook: Ideas and Activities for Building Self-Esteem.* Rochester, NY: Growth Associates.

Ellis, E. (Ed.) 1984. *Classroom Second Language Development: A Study of Classroom Interaction and Language Acquisition.* Headington Hill Hall, Oxford, England: Pergamon Press.

Enright, D.S. 1984. "The Organization of Interaction in Elementary Classrooms." In Handscombe, Jean, Richard A. Orem, and Barry P. Taylor. (Eds.) *On TESOL '83: The Question of Control.* 23-28. Washington, DC: TESOL.

Enright, D.S., and B. Gomex. 1985. "Pro-act: Six Strategies for Organizing Peer Interaction in Elementary Classrooms." *NABE Journal.* 9(3):5-24.

Enright, D.S., and M. McCloskey. 1988. *Integrating English: Developing English Language and Literacy in the Multicultural Classroom.* Reading, MA: Addison Wesley.

Enright, D.S., and M. McCloskey. 1985. "Yes Talking! Organizing the Classroom To Promote Second Language Acquisition." *TESOL Quarterly.* 19(3):431-453.

ERIC Clearinghouse on Urban Education. 1987. "Cooperative Learning in the Urban Classroom." *Equity and Choice.* 3(2):15-18.

Esling, John H. 1989. *Multicultural Education and Policy: ESL in the 1990's: A Tribute to Mary Ashworth.* Toronto, ON: OISE Press.

Fein, Greta. 1979. "Echoes from the Nursery: Piaget, Vygotsky, and the Relationship Between Language and Play." *New Directions for Child Development.* #6.

Fernandes, José. 1989. "You Can't Stop the Wind From Blowing But You Can Harness It." *OPSTF News.* April. Toronto.

Fielding, G.D., and H.D. Schalock. 1985. *Promoting the Professional Development of Teachers and Administrators.* Eugene, OR: ERIC Clearinghouse on Educational Management.

Fillmore, L. "When Does Teacher Talk Work as Input." In Gass, Susan M., and Carol G. Madden. (Eds.) 1985. *Input in Second Language Acquisition.* Rowley, MA: Newbury House.

Fillmore, L. "The Language Learner as an Individual: Implications of Research on Individual Differences for the E.S.L. Teacher." In Clarke, Mark A., and Jean Handscombe. (Eds.) 1983. *On TESOL '82: Pacific Perspectives on Language Learning and Teaching.* Washington, DC: TESOL. 157-173.

Fillmore, L. "Instructional Language as Linguistic Input: Second Language Learning Classrooms." In Wilkinson, Louise Cherry. (Ed.) 1982. *Communicating in the Classroom.* New York, NY: Academic Press.

Flores, Barbara, Patricia Tefft Cousin and Esteban Diaz. 1991. "Transforming Deficit Myths About Learning, Language, and Culture." *Language Arts.* 68 September.

Freeman, Yvonne S., and David E. Freeman. 1992. *Whole Language for Second Language Learners.* Portsmouth, NH: Heinemann Educational Books, Inc.

Gass, S.M., and C.G. Madden. (Eds.). 1985. *Input in Second Language Acquisition.* Rowley, MA: Newbury House.

Gibbs, Jeanne. 1987. *Tribes.* Santa Rosa, CA: Center Source Publications.

Goodlad, J. 1984. *A Place Called School: Prospects for the Future.* New York, NY: McGraw-Hill Book Company.

Goodman, K. 1986. *What's Whole in Whole Language.* Portsmouth, NH: Heinemann Educational Books, Inc.

Gruenewald, Lee J., and Sara A. Pollak. 1990. *Language Interaction in Curriculum and Instruction. Second Edition.* Austin, TX: Pro. Ed Publ.

Hacker, Andrew. 1992. *Two Nations.* Toronto, ON: Maxwell Macmillan Canada.

Handscombe, Jean. "Mainstreaming: Who Needs It?" In Esling, John H. (Ed.) 1989. *Multicultural Education and Policy: ESL in the 1990's.* Toronto, ON: OISE Press.

Harley, B., P. Allen, J. Cummins, and M. Swain. 1987. *The Development of Bilingual Proficiency Final Report, Vol. II.* Toronto, ON: OISE Press.

Heald-Taylor, G. 1987. *Whole Language Strategies for ESL Primary Students.* Toronto, ON: OISE Press.

Heleen, O. 1987. "Implementing Cooperative Learning: One District's Experience." *Equity and Choice.* 3(2):19-27.

Henderson, A.T., C.L. Marburger, and T. Ooms. 1986. *Beyond the Bake Sale, An Educator's Guide to Working With Parents.* Columbia, MD: National Committee for Citizens in Education.

Hester, H., 1984. "Peer Interaction in Learning English as a Second Language." *Theory Into Practice* 23(3):208-217.

Hester, H., and J. Wight. 1977. "Language in the Multi-Ethnic Classroom." *Forum.* 20(1):9-12. Autumn.

Hiebert, Elfrieda H. (Ed.) 1991. *Literacy for a Diverse Society: Perspectives, Practices and Policies.* New York, NY:. Teachers College Press. Columbia University.

Holdaway, D. 1980. *Independence in Reading.* Auckland, New Zealand: Ashton Education.

Huck, Charlotte S. "The Power of Children's Literature in the Classroom." In Short, Kathy Gnagey, and Kathryn Mitchell Pierce. (Eds.) 1990. *Talking About Books, Creating Literate Communities*. Portsmouth, NH: Heineman Educational Books, Inc.

Hudelson, Sarah. 1987. "The Role of Native Language Literacy in the Education of Language Minority Children." *Language Arts*. 64:8 December.

Hudelson, Sarah. 1984. *Kan Ye Ret an Rayt en Ingles: Children Become Literate in English as a Second Language*. TESOL Quarterly. 18(2):221-236.

Huff, Patricia, Ruth Snider and Susan Stephenson. 1986. *Teaching and Learning Skills: Celebrating Differences*. Toronto, ON: OSSTF (Ontario Secondary School Teachers' Federation).

Irving, Kathy J. 1986. *Communicating in Context*. Englewood, NJ: Prentice-Hall.

Ivic, Ivan. 1989. "Profiles of Educators: Lev S. Vygotsky." *Prospects*. 19:3.

James, R.K. 1981. "Understanding Why Curriculum Innovations Succeed or Fail." *School Science and Mathematics*. 81(6):487-495.

Johnson, Donna. 1988. "ESL Children as Teachers: A Social View of Language Use." *Language Arts*. 65(2).

Johnson, D. 1987. "The Organization of Instruction in Migrant Education: Assistance for Children and Youth at Risk." *TESOL Quarterly*. 21(3):437-459.

Jones, Pat. 1988. *Lipservice: The Story of Talk in Schools*. Philadelphia, PA: Open University Press.

Jones, R.L. (Ed.) 1976. *Mainstreaming and the Minority Child*. Minneapolis, MN: The Council for Exceptional Children.

Kagan, Spencer. 1988 Edition. *Cooperative Learning: Resources for Teachers*. Laguna Niguel, CA: University of California.

Kagan, S. 1986. "Cooperative Learning and Sociocultural Factors in Schooling." In *Beyond Language: Social and Cultural Factors in Schooling Language Minority Students*. 231-298. Los Angeles, CA: Evaluation, Dissemination and Assessment Center.

Kamil, L.K., J.A. Langer and T. Shanahan. 1985. *Understanding Research in Reading and Writing*. Newton, MA: Allyn and Bacon.

Kazalanas, J.R. 1982. "Mainstreaming: Challenge of the '80's." *Clearing House*. 55(5):199-202.

Kendall, Frances E. 1983. *Diversity in the Classroom: A Multicultural Approach to the Education of Young Children*. New York, NY: Teachers College Press.

Klippel, Friederike. 1986. *Keep Talking*. New York, NY: Cambridge University Press.

Kramsch, C. 1987. "Socialization and Literacy in a Foreign Language: Learning Through Interaction." *Theory Into Practice*. 26(4):243-250.

Krashen, Stephen. 1985. *Inquiries and Insights: Selected Essays*. Hayward, CA: Alemany Press.

Krashen, Stephen, and Tracy D. Terrell. 1983. *The Natural Approach: Language Acquisition in the Classroom*. Oxford, England: Pergamon Press.

Lee, Enid. 1985. *Letters to Marcia: A Teacher's Guide to Anti-Racist Education*. Toronto, ON: Cross-Cultural Communications Centre.

Liberman, A., and L. Miller. 1984. *Teachers, Their World, and Their Work: Implications for School Improvement.* Alexandria, VA: Association for Supervision and Curriculum Development.

Lipman, Matthew. 1991. "Squaring Soviet Theory with American Practice." *Educational Leadership.* May.

Lipson, Greta B., and Baxter Morrison. 1977. *Fact, Fantasy and Folklore: Expanding Language Arts and Critical Thinking Skills.* Carthage, IL: A Good Apple Publication.

Logan, Madge, and Cheryl Paige. 1987. "Flemington Language Project Rationale." North York, ON: Flemington Public School.

Longo, Paul. 1982. "Mainstreaming: the Promise and the Pitfalls. *Urban Education.* 17(2):157-179.

Lynch, James. 1989. *Multicultural Education in a Global Society.* New York, NY: The Falmer Press.

McCarthy, B. 1982. "Improving Staff Development Through CBAM and 4MAT." *Educational Leadership.* 40(1):20-25.

McCloskey, M. (Ed.) 1987. *Turn On Units: English as a Second Language Content Area Curriculum K-6.* Atlanta, GA: State of Georgia Board of Education.

McCurdy, J. 1983. *The Role of the Principal in Effective Schools, Problems and Solutions.* Sacramento, CA: Education News Service.

McGroarty, M. 1986. "Educators' Responses to Sociocultural Diversity: Implications for Practice." In *Beyond Language: Social and Cultural Factors in Schooling Language Minority Students.* 208-300. Los Angeles, CA: Evaluation, Dissemination and Assessment Center.

McGroarty, M. 1984. "Some Meanings of Communicative Competence for Second Language Students." *TESOL Quarterly.* 18(2):257-272.

McLaughlin, B. 1985. *Second Language Acquisition in Childhood: Vol. 2. School-Age Children.* Second Edition. Hillsdale, NJ: Lawrence Erlbaum Associates, Publishers.

McLaughlin, B. 1984. *Second Language Acquisition in Childhood: Vol. 1. Preschool Children.* Hillsdale, NJ: Lawrence Erlbaum Associates, Publishers.

Metropolitan Toronto School Board. 1988. *Together We Learn.*

Meyers, Mary. 1988. *Integration, Interaction, Interculturalism: Three Keys to Effective Mainstreaming of Second Language Students.* North York, ON. North York Board of Education.

Milk, R. 1985. "The Changing Role of ESL in Bilingual Education." *TESOL Quarterly.* 19(4):657-672.

Miller, C.H. 1987. "Ready, Set, Write!" *Equity and Choice.* (3)2:3-8.

Miller, Ron. 1991. "Defining a Common Vision." *Orbit.* 23:2. Toronto, ON: OISE Press.

Milner, David. "Children and Racism." In Keith McLeod. (Ed.) 1987. *Multicultural Education: A Partnership.* Toronto, ON: Canadian Council for Multicultural and Intercultural Education.

Moorman, C., and D. Dishon. 1983. *Our Classroom. We Can Learn Together.* Englewood Cliffs, NJ: Prentice-Hall Regents.

Moss, J.F. 1984. *Focus Units in Literature: A Handbook for Elementary School Teachers.* Urbana, IL: National Council of Teachers of English.

Murphy, Sharon. 1991. "On Skills and Whole Language." *Orbit.* Collector's Edition. Toronto, ON: OISE Press.

North York Board of Education. 1990. *Connections: Getting Ready for Co-operative Learning in Your Classroom.*

North York Board of Education. 1988. *A Framework for Progress: A Strategic Format for School and System Planning.* North York, ON: North York Board of Education.

North York Board of Education, Curriculum and Staff Development Services. 1987. *Active Learning.* North York, ON: North York Board of Education.

North York Board of Education, Curriculum and Staff Development Services. 1983. *Look! Hear!* North York, ON: North York Board of Education.

Nunan, David. 1989. *Designing Tasks for the Communicative Classroom.* New York, NY: Cambridge University Press.

Ontario Ministry of Education. 1981. *Curriculum Implementation. A Resource Booklet.* Toronto, ON: Ministry of Education.

Ontario Provincial Advisory Committee on Race Relations. 1987. *The Development of a Policy on Race and Ethnocultural Equity.* Toronto, ON: Ontario Ministry of Education.

Oracy Project. 1991. *Teaching, Talking and Learning in Key Stage Three.* Britain: National Curriculum Council Enterprises.

Pasternak, Michael G. 1979. *Helping Kids Learn Multicultural Concepts: A Handbook of Strategies.* Champaign, IL: Research Press Company.

Penfield, J. 1987. "E.S.L.: The Regular Classroom Teacher's Perspective." *TESOL Quarterly.* 21(1):21-39.

Portes, P.R. 1985. "The Role of Language in the Development of Intelligence: Vygotsky Revisited." *Journal of Research and Development in Education.* 18:4.

Purcell-Gates, Victoria. 1989. "What oral/written language differences can tell us about beginning instruction." *The Reading Teacher.* January. 290-294.

Ramsey, Patricia G. 1986. *Teaching and Language in a Diverse World.* New York, NY: Teachers College Press.

Rigg, Pat. 1991. "Whole Language in TESOL." *TESOL Quarterly.* 25:3, Autumn.

Rigg, P., and D.S. Enright. 1986. *Children and ESL: Integrating Perspectives.* Washington, DC: TESOL.

Rivers, Wilga. 1983. *Communicating Naturally in a Second Language: Theory and Practice in Language Teaching.* New York, NY: Cambridge University Press.

Rudduck, J., and D. Hopkins. (Eds.) 1985. *Research as a Basis for Teaching.* Portsmouth, NH: Heinemann Educational Books, Inc.

Samuda, R.J. (Ed.) 1986. *Multicultural Education Programmes and Methods.* Toronto, ON: Intercultural Social Sciences.

Savignon, S. 1983. *Communicative Competence: Theory and Classroom Practice.* Reading, MA: Addison-Wesley.

Saville-Troike, M. 1985. "What Really Matters in Second Language Learning for Academic Achievement." *TESOL Quarterly.* 18(2):199-219.

Schinke-Llano, L. "Foreigner Talk in Content Classrooms." In Seliger, H. W., and M.H. Long. (Eds.) 1983. *Classroom Oriented Research in Sound Language Acquisition.* Rowley, MA: Newbury House.

Schlesinger, A. 1991. "The Cult of Ethnicity, Good and Bad," *TIME* Magazine, July 8.

Schwartz, S., and M. Pollishuke. 1990. *Creating the Child-Centred Classroom.* Toronto, ON: Irwin Publishers.

Seliger, H.W., and M.H. Long. 1983. *Classroom Oriented Research in Second Language Acquisition.* Rowley. MA: Newbury House.

Semmel, M., and D. Semmel. 1979. "The Expanded Role of Regular Class Teachers." *McGill Journal of Education.* (3):327-341.

Simon, R. 1987. "Empowerment as a Pedagogy of Possibility." *Language Arts.* 64:370-383.

Simpson, M.K. 1987. "What Am I Supposed To Do While They're Writing?" *Language Arts.* 63(7):80-84.

Smagorinsky, Peter. 1991. *Expressions: Multiple Intelligences in the English Class.* Urbana, IL: National Council of Teachers of English.

Smilansky, Sara, and Leah Shefatya. 1990. *Facilitating Play: A Medium for Promoting Cognitive, Socio-Emotional and Academic Development in Young Children.* Gaithersburg, MD: Psychosocial and Educational Publications.

Sparks, Louise Derman, and the A.B.C. Task Force. 1989. *Anti-Bias Curriculum.* Washington, DC: National Association for the Education of Young Children.

Stone, Jeanne M. 1989. *Cooperative Learning and Language Arts.* San Juan Capistrano, CA: Resources For Teachers, Inc.

Swain, Merrill. 1983. "Bilingualism Without Tears." In Clarke, Mark, and Jean Handscombe. (Eds.) *On TESOL '82: Pacific Perspectives.* Washington, DC: TESOL.

Treffinger, D.J. 1982. "Gifted Students, Regular Classrooms: Sixty Ingredients for a Better Blend." *The Elementary School Journal.* 82(3):267-273.

Tunnell, Michael O., and James S. Jacobs. 1989. "Using Real Books: Research Findings on Literature Based Reading Instruction." *The Reading Teacher.* March, 470-477.

Urzua, C. 1987. "You Stopped Too Soon. Second Language Children Composing and Revising." *TESOL Quarterly.* 21(2):279-304.

Urzua, C. 1985. "How Do You Evaluate Your Own Elementary Program? Look To Kids." In Larson, Penny, Elliot L. Judd, Dorothy S. Messerschmitt (Eds.) *On TESOL '84.* 219-232. Washington, DC: TESOL.

Valdes, Joyce Merrill. (Ed.) 1986. *Culture Bound: Bridging the Cultural Gap in Language Teaching.* New York, NY: Cambridge University Press.

Ventriglia, L. 1982. *Conversations of Miguel and Maria: How Children Learn a Second Language.* Reading, MA: Addison-Wesley.

Wagner, H.S. "Kids can be ESL teachers." In Carter, Candy. (Ed.) 1982. *Non-native and non-standard dialect students.* 62-65. Urbana, IL: National Council of Teachers of English.

Wallerstein, N. 1983. *Language and Culture in Conflict: Problem-posing in the ESL Classroom.* Reading, MA: Addison-Wesley.

Walsh, Debbie. 1988. "Critical Thinking To Reduce Prejudice." *Social Education.* 52(4) April/May. 280-282.

Warren, Jean. 1984. *Storytime: Early Learning Activities.* Everett, WA: Totline Books, Warren Publishing House, Inc.

Wells, G. 1987. *Language in the Classroom: Literacy and Collaborative Talk.* Monograph Speech. Toronto, ON: OISE Press.

Wells, G. 1986. *The Meaning Makers: Children Learning Language and Using Language To Learn.* Portsmouth, NH: Heinemann Educational Books, Inc.

Wells, Gordon, and Jan Wells. 1984. "Learning To Talk and Talking To Learn." *Theory Into Practice.* Summer 23:3.

Weinberg, R., and F. Wood. (Eds.) 1975. *Observation of Pupils and Teachers in Mainstream and Special Education Settings: Alternative Strategies.* Minneapolis, MN: Leadership Training Institute.

Westby, Carol E. 1991. "Learning To Talk—Talking To Learn: Oral-Literate Language Differences." In College-Hill Press Inc. 181-210.

Wilt, Joy, and Bill Watson. 1978. *Relationship Builders Ages 4-8.* Irving, TX: Educational Products Division, Word Inc.

Wolfgang, Aaron. 1991. "Needed: Intercultural Training of Teachers and Counsellors for the Year 2000." *Orbit.* October.

Wolfgang, A. 1984. *Nonverbal Behaviour: Perspectives, Applications, Intercultural Insights.* Toronto, ON: C.J. Hogrefe.

Yalden, J. "Chicken or Egg? Communicative Methodology or Communicative Syllabus Design." In Clarke, Mark A., and Jean Handscombe (Eds.) 1983. *On TESOL '82.* 235-242. Washington, DC: TESOL.

Blackline Masters

List of Masters

BLM #1: Classroom Teacher's Strategies That Enhance Second-Language Acquisition: ATMOSPHERE

BLM #2: Classroom Teacher's Strategies That Enhance Second-Language Acquisition: PROGRAM

BLM #3: Classroom Teacher's Strategies That Enhance Second-Language Acquisition: INTERACTION

BLM #4: Background Information Sheet for a Newly Arriving ESL Student (Figure 9.2)

BLM #5: Planning Sheet for Theme-based Activity Centres (Figure 5.6)

BLM #6: Before I Make My Book

BLM #7: Book Publishing

BLM #8: Dedication and Comments from Readers Pages

BLM #9: How To Make My Own Wallpaper Book

BLM #10: Student Group Observation Sheet (Figure 8.5)

BLM #11: Alphabet Tracking Sheet (Figure 9.8)

BLM #12: Different Points of View (Figure 10.5)

BLM #13: The Problem (Figure 10.7)

How To Use Appendices #1 - #3: Classroom Teacher's List of Strategies That Enhance Second-Language Acquisition: ATMOSPHERE (#1), PROGRAM (#2), and INTERACTION (#3).

Several of the strategies overlap. They have, therefore, been reiterated with a slightly different focus, where appropriate, in all three lists.

Wait for a time when you are relaxed and can reflect without interruptions. Check off the appropriate column in the lists. Don't dwell on any one strategy too long. First impressions will suffice for the first read-through.

You will probably be surprised at all the things that you are already doing "right." This will confirm that you are on track in programming for ESL students. You will also perceive an overall impression that these strategies make sense for all the students in your class, not just for your ESL students, and that is as it should be.

These masters can be used effectively throughout the year as self-checking, self-confirming documents with which to re-evaluate your program, while at the same time, gleaning further guidance as to directions, methods and ideas to try next.

Classroom Teacher's Strategies That Enhance Second-Language Acquisition—ATMOSPHERE

In My Class I	In Use	Will Expand	Will Try
Plan instruction with a belief in providing for student success and in developing self-confidence during the process of language acquisition.			
Model a welcoming, friendly, accepting and encouraging environment and foster this approach or attitudes in my students.			
Support a risk-taking approach to using language in both oral and written tasks.			
Allow for individual rates of learning.			
Plan to develop class spirit for mutual support and group work.			
"Build bridges" between students' experiences and the Canadian milieu, e.g., shared information, country projects, folk tales, food topics, field trips, speakers from different cultures.			
Include in class displays items that reflect the multicultural and multi-racial nature of the class, e.g., pictures, languages, heritage information.			
Explicitly encourage talking and discuss it as a tool to facilitate language learning and higher level thinking skills.			
Make language useful and meaningful through activities in which students must interact in purposeful, natural settings, e.g., math centres, science experiments, field trips, problem solving.			
Familiarize new students with surroundings and staff with whom they'll be in contact.			
Encourage students to take responsibility in class, e.g., students make choices about learning tasks, design bulletin boards, change topic book display.			
Make activity centres functional. Students know where materials are kept and instructions or samples are posted for reference.			
Allocate time flexibly. Sometimes I go on "people time" as indicated by student interest as well as by "scheduled time."			

Classroom Teacher's Strategies That Enhance Second-Language Acquisition—PROGRAM

In My Class I	In Use	Will Expand	Will Try
Use visuals/concrete materials, e.g., drawings, videos, movies, props and equipment and kits.			
Include the second-language student in daily work even if he/she doesn't yet participate fully.			
Make adaptations to seatwork if necessary, e.g., draw a picture for concept or vocabulary, write in the first language, simplify vocabulary in directions.			
Provide opportunities for verbal activities, e.g., storytelling instead of story writing, report your partner's news (a new twist on an old theme), tape-recorders, discussions.			
Encourage the use of the first language with the assistance of a student or bilingual tutor to support new/abstract content. Vocabulary is easier to plug in if a concept is understood in the first language.			
Incorporate the students' first language/culture as much as possible into the ongoing curriculum, e.g., films, games, bilingual dictionaries, announcements, news bulletins, verbal and written translations.			
Actively encourage the sharing of students' thoughts on race and ethnicity in class, e.g., include questions that allow students to express their thoughts—"How were the children in the book like/not like our class?" Question to elicit thoughts on home life, family events/values. "Where do Asian/Caribbean foods fit in the Canadian food guide?" "What's the same/different in your home?"			
Develop students' awareness of one another's interests and strengths, e.g., self-esteem activities, team-building exercises.			
Ensure the involvement, interaction and collaboration of all students through the use of Cooperative Learning techniques.			
Take a cyclical approach to language experiences, content/ cognitive areas, e.g., ideas are reviewed, build on students' past experiences, ask students what they know and build from there.			
Vary group size for instruction of second-language students. The diversity of needs in large groups restrains both who gets to speak and the amount of modification to content that you can make.			
Invite students to remain with me after a lesson for further assistance or direction.			

. . . / 2

. . . / 2 PROGRAM

In My Class I	In Use	Will Expand	Will Try
Encourage all students to rely on one another for help before coming to me. Extend peer coaching beyond process writing.			
Individualize instruction and/or do comprehension checks for certain students while others are at centres or seatwork.			
Share daily reading or storytelling with students in small groups, partners and whole-class groupings.			
Support content-learning in my activity centres.			
Integrate all four language skills—reading, writing, listening and speaking—in my activity centres so as to "code" the experience in different ways for students.			
Take into account different learning styles through the variety and types of activity centres I provide. Creative and multi-sensory activities are included to develop content learning, i.e., Bloom's taxonomy.			
Allow for individual rates of learning through the range of an activity while not specifically individualizing programs, i.e., open-ended tasks.			
Look at commercially produced materials for their effect on both the comprehension and task independence factors for an ESL student, e.g., Can the student understand and do the work? Must he/she constantly rely on others for clarification?			
Include new vocabulary in weekly activities for consolidation, e.g., spelling lists, games.			
Rely on other resource people to provide input, materials or language models, e.g., speakers, librarian, special visitors, trips, consultants, volunteers.			
Stick to essential information when giving instructions.			
Keep instructions short and use simple rather than complex sentences to help focus on a task.			
Have students retell instructions.			
Don't use too many idioms without direct reference to their meanings in a context.			

. . . / 3

.../3 PROGRAM

In My Class I	In Use	Will Expand	Will Try
Frequently use comprehension checks interspersed throughout lessons.			
Accept the "silent period." I don't force language production but encourage and am receptive to student attempts.			
Correct pronunciation only as it relates to meaning/intelligibility.			
Instigate/design content-oriented activities that encourage natural social interaction, i.e., on task but interactive.			
Organize talking to elicit different types of discourse, e.g., talk for fun, to share facts or create thoughts, or problem solving.			
Include opportunities to examine people's attitudes, beliefs and values as they relate to our topics.			
Plan learning activities that relate reading and writing directly to talking and listening.			
Integrate process writing throughout the curriculum and provide feedback through conferencing opportunities.			
Include students' backgrounds in the curriculum to build self-esteem and ensure relevance to their lives, e.g., resources brought from home to support topics, sharing of information about their home lives.			
Provide time for students to play with, practise and use language at supporting materials centres, e.g., book displays, kits, equipment, models and craft supplies.			
Plan literacy instruction, i.e., reading and writing as Integrated Language Learning.			

BLM 3

Classroom Teacher's Strategies That Enhance Second-Language Acquisition—INTERACTION

In My Class I	In Use	Will Expand	Will Try
Use gestures and facial expressions to aid meaning, e.g., miming, demonstrations, use fingers to list/point. I am not afraid to ham it up.			
Use intonation/volume/pauses to aid meaning. I am expressive and play with language.			
Contextualize an idea in ways a child can relate to, on real-life experiences, e.g."...just like John did with...".			
Invite second-language students to answer by rephrasing, prompting, pausing, or rotating turn-taking.			
Rephrase or clarify a student's answer. Provide an alternative word/phrase.			
Enlarge/expand on an answer. Build on key words, concepts and student experiences.			
Ensure the repetition of key ideas or vocabulary., e.g., pattern and reuse the vocabulary in different activities.			
Speak clearly, especially when using new words of abstract meaning.			
Use shorter sentences with simplified vocabulary for newer arrivals.			
Use referential questions more than questions requiring one word or yes-no answers, i.e., ask for opinions, narratives, why and how questions.			
Encourage all students to rely on one another for help before coming to me. I extend peer help beyond process writing.			
Draw students' attention to language used in colourful, idiomatic or imaginative ways as it occurs in context.			
Use peers, older students and/or same first-language tutoring opportunities.			
Use specific techniques that generate ideas and vocabulary, e.g., brainstorming, webbing, magic circle, shared tasks, lists of new topic vocabulary.			
Provide guidance and model the appropriate language and intonation that students should use in a given context, e.g., in a student's phrasing of a question to an adult/authority figure.			
Enhance communication with parents and students by using translations and interpreters, as needed.			
Attend to racist statements.			

Background Information Sheet for a Newly Arriving ESL Student

Name _____   Date _____

Country of Birth _____   Phone _____

Arrival Date _____   Grade _____   Languages _____

Address _____   Birth Date _____

_____

A. Family Background:

Is family together? _____   Does anyone in home speak English? _____

_____

_____

(Add further details on <u>reverse</u> side.) ⟶

Languages parents/siblings are literate in _____

Health _____   Talents/Interests _____

_____

B. Previous Schooling:

_____   *Attach reports.* _____

Reads in L1 _____   Writes in L1 _____   *(Ask for student sample and attach.)* _____

Previous Exposure to English _____

Attach math sample.   Approximate Level—Needs _____

_____

_____

C. English Proficiency on Arrival   Level _____

Verbal Fluency: Can say alphabet _____   Recognizes letters _____   Matches caps & small _____

Can write alphabet _____   Knows phonics _____

Use a picture file to elicit student responses for the following:

Colours _____   Basic Verbs _____   Prepositions _____   School Vocabulary _____

Can talk about a picture in—single words/phrases/sentences *(Circle one.)* _____

Comprehends—simple directions _____, a story _____

Counts up to _____   Recognizes numbers _____   *Attach math sample.* _____

English Literacy: English reading level _____   Writes in English _____   *(Attach sample.)* _____

Assessed by _____   Date _____

_____

D. Conference/Monitoring Follow-ups *(Attach any pertinent information.)*

Date _____   Comments _____

Date _____   Comments _____

BLM 5

Planning Sheet for Theme-based Activity Centres

Enlarge on photocopier. Jot down related activities in each column. Then select and sequence the ideas in weekly plans. Highlight ideas you will need advice/help with. Cross off each area as you transfer the centres to a weekly planning sheet.

MAIN CONCEPTS	SENSORY EXPERIENCES	PERFORMING ARTS	ARTS & CRAFTS	GUESTS &/ or TRIPS
	e.g. sight, hearing, taste, touch, smell	e.g., music, creative movement, dance, demonstrations, gymnastics	e.g., mask-making, clay, design, constructions	

AUDIO-VISUAL	SHARING TIMES	DRAMA	PROBLEM SOLVING	COMPUTER PROGRAM
e.g., kits, movies, videos, TV	e.g., show & tell, collections, discussions, student presentations	e.g., skits, readers, theatre, tableaux, mime	e.g., issues, action	

STORIES/ ARTICLES	WRITING IDEAS	RELATED MATH SKILLS	ENVIRONMENTAL STUDIES	SCIENCE
			e.g., concepts, issues, materials	e.g., kits, equipment, concepts

PHONETIC & SPELLING SKILLS	NEW VOCABULARY OR TERMS	HOME ACTIVITIES	NOTES	
e.g., cross-reference with computer programs				

Before I Make My Book

1. Write my story. _____

2. Read my story to a friend.
   Does it make sense? _____

3. Ask for suggestions. _____

4. Make changes if needed. _____

5. Edit my story.

   a) Check the English _____

   b) Capitals and punctuation _____

   c) Spelling _____

6. Share my work with the teacher. _____

7. Things to do next

_____

_____

_____

_____

_____

Book Publishing

_____ 1. Decide on the type of book I want to make.

_____ 2. Put my book frame together.

_____ 3. Design my cover and title page.
Use special effects materials.

_____ 4. If my story is on the computer, cut the story up
for each page.

_____ 5. Add the background and pictures.

_____ 6. Add a "Dedications" page after my title page.

_____ 7. Add a "Comments from Readers" page at the end.

_____ 8. Arrange with the teacher to share my book.

Dedication and Comments from Readers Pages

*This Book is
Dedicated to*

_____

This page goes after
the title page.

COMMENTS
_____
from Readers

This page goes at
the back of my book.

How To Make My Own Wallpaper Book

1. Fold a piece of wallpaper in half.
   Draw a line down the middle.

2. Cut 2 pieces of cardboard.
   They must be the same size and
   they must be a bit smaller than the
   wallpaper.

3. Glue the 2 pieces of cardboard close
   to the centre of the folded sheet of
   wallpaper, but without the pieces
   of cardboard touching.

4. Fold the edges of the piece of
   wallpaper over the pieces of
   cardboard and glue.

5. The paper to go inside the book
   must be smaller than the cardboard.
   Fold the papers in half.
   Staple or sew them in the centre.

6. Glue the first page to the front cover.
   Glue the last page to the back cover.

7. Close the cover and press firmly.

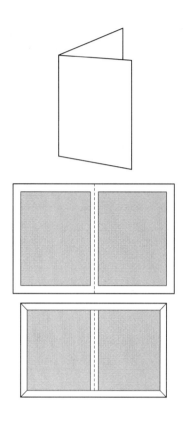

Student Group Observation Sheet

Task _____

Date _____

Group Members	Contributed Ideas	Listened to Others	_____ new skill*

COMMENTS

_____

_____

_____

_____

_____

_____

_____

_____

_____
Signature

* Takes turns, shares materials, stays on task, asks questions, summarizes ideas, helps others, etc.

Alphabet Tracking Sheet

Aa   Bb   Cc   Dd

Ee   Ff   Gg

Hh   Ii   Jj   Kk

Ll   Mm   Nn   Oo   Pp

Qq   Rr   Ss

Tt   Uu   Vv

Ww   Xx   Yy   Zz

Different Points of View

A.

_____ thinks   _____ thinks

B.   **What I Think**

_____

_____

_____

_____

_____

_____

_____

_____

_____

_____

The Problem

_____

_____

_____

_____

Solution #1

_____

_____

_____

Solution #2

_____

_____

_____

Solution #3

_____

_____

_____

Solution #4

_____

_____

_____

_____

• Which solution seems the best to you? Be prepared to say why you chose the solution you did.

• Put a red star ★ beside the solution you favour.